Inspired

Breaking the Barriers of Cultural Diversity in the Corporate World

BISMI PALATTY

First published by Ultimate World Publishing 2025
Copyright © 2025 Bismi Palatty

ISBN

Paperback: 978-1-923255-94-4
Ebook: 978-1-923255-95-1

Bismi Palatty has asserted her rights under the Copyright, Designs and Patents Act 1988 to be identified as the author of this work. The information in this book is based on the author's experiences and opinions. The publisher specifically disclaims responsibility for any adverse consequences which may result from use of the information contained herein. Permission to use information has been sought by the author. Any breaches will be rectified in further editions of the book.

All rights reserved. No part of this publication may be reproduced, stored in or introduced into a retrieval system, or transmitted in any form, or by any means (electronic, mechanical, photocopying, recording or otherwise) without the prior written permission of the author. Any person who does any unauthorised act in relation to this publication may be liable to criminal prosecution and civil claims for damages. Enquiries should be made through the publisher.

Cover design: Ultimate World Publishing
Layout and typesetting: Ultimate World Publishing
Editor: Rebecca Low
Cover Image Copyright: MiTo Design-Shutterstock.com

Ultimate World Publishing
Diamond Creek,
Victoria Australia 3089
www.writeabook.com.au

Dedication

To all migrants who left their home country for a better life.

Contents

Dedication iii
Introduction: A Migrant's Journey: *Finding My Voice* 1
Chapter 1: Centring on Core Values: *The Cornerstone of Success* ... 3
Chapter 2: Cultural Competence: *Cultivating a Global Mindset* ... 13
Chapter 3: Conscious and Unconscious Bias:
    Mitigating Workplace Inequalities 23
Chapter 4: Cultivating Commitment: *Igniting Your Inner Fire* ... 37
Chapter 5: Conquer Your Fear: *Championing Confidence* 51
Chapter 6: Cooperative Synergy:
    Driving Shared Vision Through Collaboration 63
Chapter 7: Commitment to Continuous Growth:
    Future-Proofing Your Career 75
Chapter 8: Competitive Growth Mindset:
    Outsmart, Outplay, Outshine 85
Chapter 9: Criteria for Promotion Clarified:
    Your Career, Your Roadmap 97
Chapter 10: Constructing Clear Boundaries:
    Setting Limits, Reaching Heights 109
Chapter 11: Cultivating Career Aspirations:
    Investing in Human Capital 121
Chapter 12: Commemorating Achievements:
    More Than Milestones, a Celebration of You 135
About the Author 147

Introduction

A Migrant's Journey: *Finding My Voice*

I may not have all the answers, but I've learned a thing or two along the way. My journey as a migrant has been marked by challenges, triumphs, and a profound sense of self-discovery. I've lost touch with my cultural roots, struggled with family dynamics, and faced the isolation that comes with being an outsider.

I spent years wandering, chasing fleeting goals and sacrificing my well-being. It wasn't until I hit rock bottom that I realised the importance of personal growth, resilience, and cultural identity. I had wasted precious time and energy, neglected my relationships, and compromised my happiness by running behind corporate dreams with a migrant mindset.

I remember the day I felt like giving up. I was overwhelmed by the challenges I faced, both personally and professionally, but something inside me refused to surrender. It was at that moment that I discovered a strength I never knew I possessed. Yet, through it all, I've found strength, resilience, and a renewed sense of purpose. I've learned the importance of connecting with my core, embracing my cultural identity, and advocating for myself. This book is a demonstration of my journey, a story of overcoming adversity and finding my voice.

What does it mean to truly be culturally diverse? Is it about achieving material success or climbing the ladder and creating the best life for you? I believe it's about fostering a sense of belonging, understanding, and respect for others. It's about creating a more inclusive and equitable society where everyone feels valued and empowered. The world is full of obstacles, but they're not insurmountable. With the right mindset and the determination to succeed, we can overcome any challenge and achieve these dreams.

This is an autoethnographic exploration of my migration story. I don't want you to make the same mistakes I did. I want you to know how I passed and what helped me transform myself. I acknowledge that little knowledge is dangerous, but this experience made me believe I'm unique and have a purpose in this life. That was the starting point of my learning. I hope my experiences **inspire** and empower other migrants like you to break free from the invisible barriers that hold us back. Together, we can challenge stereotypes, advocate for equity, and create a more inclusive environment. I'm continuing my journey and evolving myself at all levels, including my corporate career goals. Let's embark on this journey together, exploring the depths of your being and unlocking your extraordinary potential. You can create a life of freedom, fulfillment, and purpose by understanding yourself, embracing your unique qualities, cultivating resilience, and connecting to spirituality. Breaking the barriers in your mindset is the best way to get a breakthrough in your corporate dreams.

'Connecting to core is the beginning of change'

Chapter 1

Centring on Core Values: The Cornerstone of Success

'In the beginning, God created the heavens and Earth' (Genesis 1:1). I'm fortunate to start my life in God's own country. My life started small, like a mango seed in a cosy little world. Back home in India, everything felt right. The rhythm of the seasons, the taste of homemade food, the laughter of friends, and our community's gentle hum were all comfortingly familiar.

My family and our community were blessed. Our lives were simple but fully busy with different activities. We had enough to eat, a roof over our heads, and love to warm our hearts. I still remember the day our first television arrived in our house; it was like a miracle. Our home became the centre of the village on match days, with neighbours crowding in, their eyes glued to the small screen. I was busy serving coffee and snacks, and, in those moments, I felt like I was hosting a grand event. I was also proud because the television was a reward from my dad for achieving good grades in year 10, and it was inspiring to see that people were enjoying the sports they love.

Life was good, or so I thought. The future was a clear path: school, college, teaching, marriage, and children. It was a blueprint handed down from generations, and I unquestioningly followed it. I was told becoming a teacher was my destiny—a life scripted not by passion but by expectation. My parents were teachers, so it was only natural that I would become one as well. Like a little bird learning to fly by copying its mother, I thought that's what I was supposed to do. Though I loved teaching, I was still thinking about why my parents didn't ask me to think in another way or was it my responsibility to think outside the box?

I was that frog in the pond who thought its world was the lily pad. I was happy in my little corner and unaware of the vast ocean beyond. I still remember a cute song my mum sang about little frogs and ponds, where they thought it was the only big world and they were the luckiest. Thus, like all other people in that small village, I followed the path laid out for me as it seemed like the natural order and my only option. I was content, but deep down, a tiny voice whispered, 'Is this all there is?'

Back home, life was small, familiar, and not so quiet, but it was comfortable and predictable. The days and nights had their worries, but this little world wasn't highly impacted by anything. I was hoping that marriage was like adding another lily pad to that peaceful world. Then came the decision to move to Australia, a leap from that familiar pond into the vast, stormy ocean. Excitement bubbled like a frog on a sunny day, but soon reality hit like a cold splash. This was no longer a gentle pond but a churning sea full of unfamiliar currents and creatures.

Before migrating in 2000, I didn't know much about Australia besides kangaroos and the lack of spicy food ingredients. Our luggage was a

Centring on Core Values: The Cornerstone of Success

mix of spices, Indian cooking pots, and some Western clothes. There weren't many brown people in the place where we migrated. I used to look for them in shopping centres and trains and try to find out whether they were from Asian countries. But now things have changed a lot.

Being a migrant, I was fortunate that I had a house to live in and good, tasty food from my sister-in-law. I was thinking that the migration of life would be easy and smooth. But the cold logic of the job market was a stark contrast to the warmth of my familiar world. The world told me my math degree was a dead-end here. It was like being handed a useless tool in a foreign land. With no further knowledge to communicate and investigate, I had to listen to my family's wisdom, which is why we should be living as a family. To survive, I had to reinvent myself and become a digital expert. I was forced to be a student again, not just in the classroom but in the harsh school of life as well. It was an unexpected detour that Australia gave me. I blindly followed a path and disconnected from my core compass. Or did I even have a compass to guide me? Something was missing, a piece of me that didn't quite belong here.

The completion of my IT studies filled me with anticipation for a fulfilling career in Australia's corporate landscape. The initial excitement of a new beginning transformed into a bleak reality. The concept of core values seemed a distant luxury. Every interaction was a battle, a constant struggle against the tide of unfamiliarity. I felt like a fish out of water, gasping for air in a world that didn't understand me. Survival was the primary focus—finding a job in the area I mastered, securing a home, and mastering the intricacies of a foreign language. Amid this struggle, the idea of identifying personal values felt like an indulgence.

My accent, though melodious to my ears, was a melody unfamiliar to Australian ears and was met with impatience and misunderstandings. With each passing day, my confidence eroded, replaced by a growing sense of isolation. The world I had known, with its strong sense of community and shared values, seemed distant. The family I was leaning on for help didn't know what to do. Many unfamiliar customs and expectations from all different areas of my life took me down. People often mistook my silence for indifference and hesitancy for arrogance. The world seemed divided into two: those who looked at me with curiosity and those with outright hostility.

I vividly recall my first Australian barbecue. It was my first month in Melbourne, and we were at our cousin's house. The sight of raw meat sizzling on a metal plate was alien to me. Trying to enjoy half-cooked meat mixed with leaves felt like a culinary challenge. My first Australian English-speaking guest, along with family, turned this social gathering into a linguistic minefield; I was going into my shell and becoming a silent observer. The forced introduction to a stranger, coupled with my desperate attempt to impress, created a perfect storm of anxiety.

The pressure to impress was immense. Introduced as a master's graduate, I felt like a fraud when faced with a simple conversation. Understanding Aussie English was harder than coding in different computer languages. She asked me different things, and I didn't understand a single word from her. At the end of her questions, I gave my first speech to her in grammatical English, telling her the story of my degree and my current job-seeking experience. My carefully constructed English response wasn't related to the conversation, and the laughter that followed my attempt at polite conversation was a stinging reminder of my inadequacy. I never saw her again, but the experience motivated me to learn and understand Aussie English, so I'm thankful to her for listening to me without intimidating responses.

That night, I realised the gap between my world and this new reality. I was a stranger in a strange land, desperately trying to find my footing. It was a humbling experience, a painful initiation into the harsh realities of migration. Radio, television, and newspapers became my

Centring on Core Values: The Cornerstone of Success

new companions. I learned that family, while a source of support, can also be a double-edged sword. Their expectations and advice, while well-intentioned, sometimes hindered my progress. It was a solitary journey filled with both challenges and triumphs. Has anyone else felt this isolation and confusion when first arriving in a new country?

A master's degree felt like a crown I'd earned, a testament to years of hard work. But in this new land, it was worthless to me. I was a skilled professional in one world and a lost soul in another. All the interview responses I received said that I was overqualified for entry-level work, which was a dagger to my pride. My family's suggestion to 'think bigger and do better' was a cruel irony. Bigger thoughts needed a language to take flight, but English here was a foreign dialect to me.

My first job in this country was as a baker's helper. Each slice of bread was a cut to my dignity. The years of study I did by sacrificing my family life and the dreams of a fulfilling career seemed to crumble with every loaf. Was it my accent, skin, or naivety that condemned me to this? The weight of loneliness pressed down, heavier than the dough I kneaded.

I became a ghost, existing but unseen. My spirit, once vibrant, was now a muted echo. The simple act of picking up my boss's suit from the dry cleaners felt like a surrender, a silent acceptance of my diminished status. I didn't know how to speak up for my core values. I was a pawn in a game I didn't understand, a puppet with severed strings. I was drowning in a sea of self-doubt, a prisoner in my own life. The weight of expectations, both self-imposed and societal, pressed down on me.

Landing my first IT job after 18 months of solo hurdles felt like a dream realised. It was a testament to my university tutor's belief in my abilities. Their guidance was instrumental in securing a role that aligned with my studies. To gain deeper industry experience, I pursued further studies in Australia. While this path seemed logical at the time, I hadn't fully explored my personal or professional values. My sole focus was immersing myself in the IT world and building a better family.

Finding my footing as a migrant in a new corporate world wasn't an easy task for me. I didn't realise early on the importance of understanding my core values to stay grounded. I was a totally different person at work. I just did the work that was assigned and didn't really talk to anyone. At home, I became a different soul with a different purpose. Since I worked for a big company, it was often unclear what was truly expected. Was it just about completing tasks, or was there a deeper purpose? I'd often find myself questioning my role and impact. It was like being a cog in a machine, blindly following instructions without understanding the bigger picture. This autopilot mode continued for a long time to ensure I survived in this new, unknown world. Improving my family's well-being was a priority, but I didn't achieve success there either.

Nine years ago, my world turned upside down. A seemingly ordinary day in the busy hospital I worked at took a terrifying turn for me. A colleague noticed an unusual tremor in my face, a silent alarm that foreshadowed a crisis. What followed was a blur of medical tests and diagnoses. Cerebral aneurysm—the words echoed in my mind like a death sentence. The shame and guilt of all the hidden situations were unveiled that day. That was when I felt I shouldn't be hiding things from my workplace. Being a single parent of my 14-month-old twins and seven-year-old son, I didn't have anyone to call for help other than the only family who helped me in the saga of single parenting. The decision to undergo risky surgery was the only choice for me to save my life. The thought of leaving my children without a mother was unbearable. Yet, I was trapped in a nightmare of my own making. Years earlier, I'd fled a toxic relationship to protect my sons from harm. It was a decision born out of love and desperation, a choice that had isolated me.

Centring on Core Values: The Cornerstone of Success

Migrants always feel nervous when they get phone calls about their loved ones from their town. I used to get phone calls only for sad news those days, and the worst was the call from my dad saying he was having severe issues that needed urgent surgery. I couldn't be there with my family for my brother's wedding celebrations and even to support my mother when she had a stroke. All the excuses were financial struggles or horrible employers who wouldn't give them leave. But this time, I could decide as I was the sole decision maker, and I had that gut feeling to see my hero, my dad, before my risky surgery.

So, I went to see my dad, who was also having surgery to remove his tumour, with the help of a full-time family carer who looked after my boys for just four days. The surgery was a success, but the patient was going to die; that was great news waiting for me when I landed back in Australia. The news of my dad's sudden death opened up another traumatic situation to answer the community about my separation and all the unacceptable behaviour that I was doing at that time. The emotional turmoil I endured during those days in Australia is almost indescribable. Isolation, fear, and uncertainty were my constant companions. As a solitary migrant, I couldn't experience any empathy or help from my community and family. I felt safe to be alone and keep it in myself. Everyone was finding different ways to poke my emotions which helped me to become more independent and make my own decisions. Did I miss any other help that was available during that time? I doubt it.

The amazing surgeons at my workplace were the angels who helped me to breathe again and I'm always grateful to those who were in my journey. The road to recovery was long and arduous. I emerged from the experience with a newfound appreciation for life, a fierce determination to protect my children, and a burning desire to create a better future for them. I wanted to raise sons who understood empathy, respect, and kindness. It was a daunting task, but I embraced this great love for some time. But, juggling being a single parent with different medical issues and a demanding corporate job took a toll on my personal and career aspirations.

I became more focused on financial survival than personal fulfillment. The initial excitement of starting a new life in Australia soon faded into a fog of isolation. Professionally, I felt invisible. My qualifications, once a source of pride, seemed irrelevant in this new landscape. The constant feeling of being an outsider chipped away at my self-esteem. Different decisions and role changes happened with no real goals and no alignment with my values. I was thinking that everyone was showing me different faces. Everyone was taking advantage of my skills and backstabbing me. Everyone was showing discrimination because of my colour, accent, way of doing things, body image, and communication style. I found myself blaming external factors for my struggles, overlooking the deeper issues within. It was a painful realisation that true growth required self-reflection and a willingness to confront my own shortcomings.

A perfect storm of personal and global crises shook me to my core. Health scares and the loss of loved ones collided with the chaos of the pandemic, forcing me to re-evaluate everything. This personal crisis became a catalyst for self-discovery, and I embarked on a journey to reconnect with my core values and find true purpose, seeking solace in spirituality and self-love. It would take not only a journey across continents but different personal and professional crises to truly understand the depth of my own being. I started to realise that I needed to find my core, my true self. It was time to stop being a passive observer and become the captain of my own ship. Little did I know that the world was a vast ocean, and I was just a drop of water, unaware of the currents that could carry me to distant shores.

So that's where I started to understand the power of self-love, which helped me find out the real soul and spirituality and identify the meaning of the status quo we're maintaining. It's the real one, the authentic one you're building up in and around your community through small gestures

Centring on Core Values: The Cornerstone of Success

of love, peace and joy. It all starts when you start loving yourself and your core. Reflecting on our own purpose and values is the key element I was missing all these years. I didn't work intentionally towards my values; I was just drifting towards some passion with no direction. What I learned is that whatever your career is, whoever the employer is, growth and success depend on your core values and your connection to them.

How can you identify and align those values? What were the next questions in my life? The current digital world offers a wealth of information, but true wisdom comes from within because your journey is unique, and you need to sit down and reflect on your life. I have four sets of questions I used to ask myself to set the values for me and my family:

1. Define Your Values Clearly:
    - What do these values truly mean to me?
    - How are they evident in my life?
    - Are there specific behaviours or actions associated with these values in me?
2. Evaluate Your Current Life:
    - How aligned are my current actions and decisions with my values?
    - Are there areas where I'm compromising my values?
    - What changes can I make to bring my life more into alignment?
3. Set Goals:
    - How can I incorporate my values into my goals?
    - What steps can I take to live more authentically?
4. Regular Reflection:
    - Schedule time for self-reflection to assess my progress.
    - Am I making choices that honour my values?
    - Are these values evolving in my life?

Tools for Self-Discovery

- o Journaling: Write about your thoughts, feelings, and experiences.
- o Meditation or Mindfulness: Cultivate inner peace and clarity.
- o Values Assessments: Online tools can provide a starting point.
- o Life Coaching: Seek professional guidance, and if you think I can help you, connect with me.

Utilise the tools available around you, but also connect with your core and pick the top three values you care about so you can work towards them. This will change your work-life perception and become the foundation of success. I realised that I'm a beautifully and wonderfully made unique masterpiece, and I have a purpose in this world to spread love, joy and peace. Yes, that's what I'm doing through my life and work. I'm restored to a better version of myself now and still evolving.

Chapter 2

Cultural Competence: *Cultivating a Global Mindset*

'Take courage, my girl,' a faint whisper echoed in my mind many times. Yet, in the desolate landscape of my negative mindset, action felt impossible. I know 'my Creator has the plans for me, plans for welfare and not for evil, to give me a future and hope.' But it took years to understand that the experiences we have in life, whether good or bad, have many things to teach us, and they happen for a reason. I have to cultivate my mindset through these experiences rather than discover the pessimism there.

Arriving in Australia in 2000 marked the commencement of a new chapter in my life. The western suburbs of Melbourne were then predominantly inhabited by individuals of Anglo-Celtic heritage, with Indian faces a rare sight. Outward appearances, such as attire, gait, and even language, often drew curious and sometimes disapproving glances in public spaces, from places of worship to commercial hubs. However, by 2024, the nation has transformed into a vibrant mosaic of cultures, with a substantial surge in populations from Asia, India, and the Middle East.

I used to gaze at brown faces and was so happy to connect with them to share the solitude I was feeling at that time. Sometimes, they were also in similar desolation and didn't make many connections. We used to share a sense of isolation, and these encounters revealed a mutual loneliness and a yearning for connection. Even though we were united by our Indian heritage, we navigated the challenges of linguistic and cultural barriers, and our conversations were often patchworked with broken phrases and gestures. It was hard to continue these connections with the different family setups.

Connecting with the local library was my initial step as a new immigrant—the great advice we used to get from other migrants. As a teacher (who isn't accredited in Australia for teaching) with a master's degree in computer applications, I found an opportunity to teach seniors at a community centre, which was my first experience of local culture. The elderly women showed warmth and kindness, and their enthusiasm for mastering Microsoft Word and Outlook was contagious. I felt privileged to guide these amazing individuals in their new phase of life. I wonder why I didn't connect with them after leaving those places.

The Overseas Qualified Professionals Program became a hub for connecting with fellow migrants from diverse backgrounds, including a few from my hometown. These initial acquaintances blossomed into deep friendships, fostering a strong support network. Together, we navigated the complexities of the Australian corporate landscape, sharing knowledge and experiences. The people from our hometown started to grow and connect as a community to cultivate our culture and traditions.

Cultural Competence: Cultivating a Global Mindset

But this program or preparation didn't give me enough of an idea of regular Australian idioms used in the corporate world. A recent meeting proved to be a valuable learning experience. Our Australian team lead outlined the new project strategy, confidently stating, 'We need to line up the ducks before we launch.' The entire Australian team nodded in agreement, but I was perplexed, envisioning an actual parade of ducks. Hesitant to inquire about these feathered creatures, I remained silent. Subsequent discussions failed to clarify the matter. After the meeting, I resorted to Google and discovered that 'lining up the ducks' was a metaphorical expression for organising tasks. This incident highlighted the importance of cultural immersion, emphasising the need to engage with Australian media and colleagues. While initially embarrassing, these misunderstandings facilitated deeper connections, bridging the gap between cultures and fostering a better understanding of Australian slang and idioms.

All idioms have different reasoning and stories behind them. The saying 'lining up all your ducks' or 'getting all your ducks in a row' means to organise or arrange things in a neat and orderly manner, often in preparation for a particular task or event. It suggests being well-prepared and having everything in place to achieve a goal or deal with a situation effectively. The phrase can be from the image of a mother duck leading her ducklings in a row while swimming or may have originated from the world of hunting terminology. Knowing the real reason for using these idioms gives them a deeper meaning.

I was reading the explanation that when lying in a punt on a lake, with a massive punt gun, you had to be extremely patient to wait until you had 'lined up the decoys', same as a line of ducks, before pulling the trigger in order to make the hunt worthwhile. This took me into the vast space of Australian history. I realised it was a big mistake that I missed all the favourite Australian TV series like *Kath and Kim*, *Home and Away*, and *Neighbours*. I'm so grateful for my Australian peers and these misunderstandings at the workplace. They helped me to invest myself in a new area of knowledge and understand more about the culture. After all these years, I'm still not a pro in Australian idioms and slang, but the basic must-know ones are regular in conversations with my teenage boys. Arvo, barbie, bikkie, brekkie, bloke, footy, and Maccas are in my regular conversation and you can give it a go too!

Twenty years ago, the Australian corporate world wasn't the same as it is now. There were no harmonious days or multi-cultural celebrations at your workplace. The first and last experience of embracing cultural diversity was the team building exercise we had outside the workplace. The CEO of that private organisation was so eager to experience something different that we opted to have a traditional Indian dinner. I was eager to share all the different sarees from my suitcase with my Australian colleagues, and I was the stylist who draped the sarees for them. We had a great experience of sharing love and joy. That was the first time I felt that cultures can connect in different ways to improve your confidence and competence. However, moving to other workplaces made it hard to feel the same spirit.

Different organisations have an array of cultures, and connecting to people from different backgrounds is never the same. In some places, the aroma of my home-cooked Asian meal, a comforting familiarity to me, seemed to be a source of discomfort for some. The unspoken pressure to conform to Australian lunch norms was a constant undercurrent, stifling my authenticity. Some colleagues showed obvious discrimination—their opinions were evident in their actions, speech, and even written communication. While legally prohibited, these discriminatory acts often occurred with tacit approval from leadership. It became apparent that the mindset of senior executives mirrored the discriminatory attitudes prevalent among lower-level employees.

Everyone was busy in their own world or their own small bubbles where no one was invited. I felt like we needed something new to connect with others and try different ideas. The multicultural lunch events and coffee breaks that were done at different times didn't share a real cultural diversity spirit. These events lacked genuine purpose and failed to create a positive impact on the inclusion mindset. I retreated into my shell, consumed by self-doubt and questioning the effectiveness of my efforts to build the cultural mindset.

Demonstrating respect for cultural diversity and inclusion while embracing all nationalities is essential for cultivating a global perspective. As an Indian, I recognise that many cultural norms and traditions are deeply rooted in a colonial mindset, making change challenging. Addressing one's superior with deference, standing up as a sign of respect, and using titles like 'Sir' and 'Madam' are customary practices.

When we leave our country for a reason, we're not leaving the culture. But that shouldn't be a barrier to a global mindset of accepting all cultures, especially in the country we currently live in. Bias is a universal challenge, but the true obstacle to overcoming it lies within the migrant's own mindset. Changing a deeply ingrained mindset is a complex process, but it's achievable with conscious effort and rewiring our brains. We need to identify these changes and modify them according to the culture we belong to now. Cultural competence is the ability to understand, appreciate and effectively interact with people from diverse cultural backgrounds. We have to start with our conscious efforts by learning more about the culture, respecting cultural differences, and promoting inclusivity. It's a continuous learning process and reflection of our own self and our progression in connecting with people from different cultures. Empathy and open-mindedness are key for migrants to improve their mindset.

Embracing a new culture doesn't necessitate abandoning one's heritage. As an Indian woman, I cherish wearing traditional attire and adorning my forehead with a bindi. I've had to answer the reason for wearing this bindi to different people, including in interviews, and was surprised by how people appreciate the culture of having different styles of bindi. It's my tradition that I love to follow as it's a symbol of respect for my husband, family, and in-laws. This tradition continues to inspire me, demonstrating that cultural connection can be maintained in any way we feel comfortable.

Wearing ashes on Ash Wednesday is indeed a visible expression of faith and identity for many Christians. It's a tangible way to connect with your spiritual beliefs and share them with the world. Being a Catholic, I'm proud to share my beliefs by wearing ashes on my forehead. Participating in the Anzac Day dawn service with family is a powerful way to respect Australian history while celebrating Onam with my community preserves my cultural heritage and ensures its continuity for future generations. It's a wonderful example of how one can be a proud custodian of Australian culture while embracing a new home. It's a beautiful way to honour both our heritage and adopted country. As an Indian attending a cricket match between Australia and India at the Melbourne Cricket Ground, who would you support? This perfectly encapsulates the enduring power of your cultural identity.

I was touched by a connection with an Indigenous community member recently. I can connect the way they used to listen to their grandparents and their storytelling styles when I listened to stories and connections. I can feel a deep connection between Indigenous people and the land and a similar attachment to our homeland and communities. It was a perspective that resonated with my Indian roots, where reverence for nature and ancestors is deeply ingrained. That's when I started to think and experience the power of acknowledging the country of Australia and why we should feel the love while sharing the acknowledgment. It's not just a mandatory practice, but the heartfelt connection between the culture we're now part of and our own deep-rooted culture.

It was a long journey filled with challenges and self-doubt. But my mindset transformation was a testament to the resilience I had. I tried to overcome the language barrier through different learning options available but also embraced a new culture, creating a harmonious blend in my life. New ideas and thoughts used to come to mind while connecting with people from different cultures; the customs, traditions, values, and vision all started to make sense in my life. This ongoing journey is helping me learn about the uniqueness of each culture and, at the same time, the authenticity of my Indian culture.

The fear of rejection was replaced by a sense of belonging and curiosity. I started to appreciate the beauty of Australian landscapes, the friendliness of the people, and the country's multicultural fabric. Enjoying the green pastures, cold foggy drives, autumn leaves and great spring blooms, made me feel a deep connection to this new home. The vast, open skies and the rhythmic crash of waves against the shore offered a tranquillity that soothed my soul. Hiking through the bush, camping under a canopy of stars, and simply sitting by the beach watching the sunset became my escapes, my moments of pure bliss. Australia, with its raw natural beauty and welcoming spirit, had captured my heart in my solitary life.

Exploring Victoria with family was like discovering a treasure of natural wonders. The Great Ocean Road, with its dramatic cliffs and the mesmerising Twelve Apostles, left me breathless. The mysterious styles of Buchan Caves unveiled an underground world of wonder. The serenity of the Lakes Entrance offered a peaceful retreat amidst nature's embrace. The snowy mountains beckoned for discovery, and long drives between states were unforgettable adventures filled with encounters with kangaroos, wallabies, and towering trucks. The vibrant energy of the city of Melbourne was a constant source of eagerness. The city's rhythm, marked by the rumble of trains, the slow crawl of buses, and long drives across the West Gate Bridge, became a familiar soundtrack to my life. Even the iconic pier, with its bustling activity of yachts and sailboats gliding across the water, added vibrant colours to my visual experience. Each journey was a step closer to understanding the heart of this beautiful country.

Inspired

The rich variety of flavours from around the world added another layer of enchantment. The vibrant coffee culture, from the velvety smooth latte to the bold espresso, was a new indulgence. The diverse food scene was a culinary adventure, and different cuisines offered tempting new tastes. But it was the unexpected delights that truly captured my heart—the crispy texture of dimsims, the fiery kick of Thai curry, the rich depth of Italian pasta, the delicate sweetness of French pastries, and the comforting warmth of Indian curries. These experiences, combined with the warmth of the Australian people, created a sense of belonging and contentment I had never imagined possible. I came to the realisation that cultural integration takes time, so I have to be patient with myself and enjoy the process of learning and growing. It's not a destination; it's a journey, and I was enjoying it with my three wonderful boys.

Ultimately, cultural competence is about building bridges between different cultures, fostering mutual understanding, and creating inclusive environments. Through all these experiences, I'm still learning that cultural awareness is the core of cultural competency, which is the ability to recognise and appreciate the differences and similarities between cultures. If I'm culturally competent, I should be able to interact effectively with people from different cultures with ease and respect and appreciate other cultures. So, I need to focus on understanding that people from different backgrounds have diverse values, beliefs, and customs. That's the reason I'm trying to practise these key components of cultural awareness.

- Recognising your own personal cultural biases.
- Respecting the diversity we experience in the country we're living.
- Seeking help to understand and learn from other cultures by making connections.
- Adapting and adjusting communication styles to suit current cultural context.

Cultural Competence: Cultivating a Global Mindset

What can we do to create a global cultural mindset, and do you feel that it's not practical in our busy day-to-day lives? What I used to do was check these statements and score myself to determine whether I could answer yes to at least five things. If NOT, I would work towards the areas that were closer to me to act on. You can be a master of enjoying the wonderful multicultural world of any country. It starts with YOU. So, rate your cultural competency here:

1. Be curious to know about other cultures and traditions.
2. Embrace the Aussie slang: learning common Aussie phrases can make you feel more connected. (If you're not in Australia, find out the local slang from the country you're in).
3. Participate in local events and festivals: this is a great way to immerse yourself in the culture.
4. Participate in more than one cultural group outside of work.
5. Be involved in workplace initiatives related to cultural diversity.
6. Participate in local holidays and activities (like ANZAC and Remembrance Day) and learn about the history of those days.
7. Be involved in any local groups (with Indigenous people if you're in Australia) or activities around you.
8. Learn about the country's own style of music, art, and facts.
9. Find out more about the country you live in and identify the importance of the place you live/work.
10. Be friends with people from different cultures and share your culture (start with food).

11. Be yourself: authenticity is always appreciated, so be true to yourself while embracing new experiences.
12. Be inspired by the variety of culture and goodness we have in the country we're in.

Chapter 3

Conscious and Unconscious Bias: Mitigating Workplace Inequalities

In Australia, women have made gradual progress in reaching C-level roles in the last 20 years, even though they remain underrepresented. As of 2023, women hold about 19.4% of CEO positions and 34.5% of key management personnel roles. Over the past decade, there has been a modest increase in these numbers, but the growth rate has been slow—roughly four percentage points in nine years. Even though organisations showcase higher rates of women in leadership, they're not ready to admit that there are very few brown leaders in their cohort. Other than that, the period for an ordinary person to move from entry-level jobs to these higher levels is huge, even if they're ready to sacrifice their personal and family life.

Inspired

My 15 years navigating Australia's healthcare system have unveiled a maze of internal politics, rivalries, bullying, and cutthroat competition that disproportionately hinder migrant advancement to leadership roles. These obstacles are often worsened by factors such as managerial favouritism, undervalued foreign qualifications, language hurdles hindering clear communication, and the absence of local connections. Without influential sponsors, even the most skilled and high-performing migrants find upward mobility elusive. The unspoken truth is that migrants must exert twice the effort of their male Caucasian counterparts to gain recognition and career progression. This begs the question: despite India's technological competence, why are Indian executive directors so scarce? My two-decade career has yielded no Asian directors, leaving me pondering an elusive yet crucial, missing element.

Research shows migrants, usually concentrated in lower-level roles in the IT world and health sector area, face slower career progression than their Australian-born peers. In my community, the migrants who became leaders were mostly males. Conversations with highly qualified and skilled female leaders opened up the fact that the competitive mindset among leadership teams always takes a toll on them. Since it's hard to put boundaries on their heart, many incidents will impact their confidence and self-esteem.

Then, they're trying to channel their leadership qualities to the areas where they or their families benefit. I can see migrant female leaders starting their own small businesses or running community-oriented leadership or church-related teams. They're comfortable with having a good balance in the workplace and exploring leadership qualities in other areas. This is taking them into an unconscious bias at the workplace that they may not even feel or acknowledge.

According to a report by the Australian Human Rights Commission and various studies, migrants, particularly those from non-English speaking backgrounds, experience significant barriers to career progression. This is partly due to systemic barriers like unconscious and conscious bias in hiring and promotion practices. The experience of a young Indian Human Resource specialist who did her studies here in Australia is very alarming. While her sector across organisations is facing high demand, her experience repeatedly reveals that race is a barrier to employment due to its perceived connection with various individuals within the company.

To truly grasp the mindset of the applicant pool, it's imperative to have first-generation migrants represented in these departments. Teams lacking in both first-generation migrants and female members are prone to biased decisions and practices during the hiring process, ultimately harming the entire organisation. Public organisations often have stringent policies in place regarding the hiring of permanent residents for leadership positions. However, it's important to recognise that some of these rules may be rooted in biased decisions made by previous leadership teams. While it's encouraging to see occasional case-by-case modifications that allow for the selection of the best candidate, regardless of their residency status, it's disheartening to observe that those headhunted often belong to the Caucasian demographic or their social circles. This perpetuates a system that favours certain groups over others, hindering diversity and inclusion within leadership roles.

It's taking time to implement the idea of intersectionality and diversity in the workplace and my experience is that many middle-class employees won't benefit, so they're hesitant to make any changes. Are we consciously looking into these areas at the workplace to support intersectionality and diversity?

> A. Recognising that a woman of colour may face unique challenges and discrimination due to her race and gender.
>
> B. Understanding that a person with a disability who is also LGBTQ+ may face additional barriers and discrimination due to the combination of their identities.

C. Acknowledging that a working-class individual may face challenges in accessing opportunities and resources due to their socioeconomic status, regardless of their other identities.

D. Can we create safe spaces for these employees to discuss their concerns and experiences without feeling dismissed or invalidated?

E. Are we utilising the data on employee demographics and analysing it through an intersectional lens to identify specific barriers and challenges different groups face within the organisation?

F. Are we fostering a workplace culture that values and celebrates diversity in all its forms by encouraging open dialogue, active listening, and empathy among employees?

By adopting an intersectional approach, organisations can create a more inclusive and equitable workplace for all employees, regardless of their background or identity. While it's important to acknowledge the specific challenges marginalised groups face, it's equally important not to overlook the experiences of those who may not fall into easily defined categories. The 'middle-class bunch' may experience unique challenges and biases that aren't always recognised or addressed.

Many Asian migrants arrive in Australia shouldering significant financial burdens, driven by the noble goal of supporting their families back home. This often translates into a strong work ethic and a willingness to take on demanding jobs. However, the reality of the corporate sector can be disillusioning. The path to high-paying positions is often riddled with obstacles, and securing a substantial income can be a protracted struggle. This financial pressure, coupled with the challenges of navigating a new culture and potentially restrictive migrant laws, can lead to significant stress and burnout.

Conscious and Unconscious Bias: Mitigating Workplace Inequalities

Some migrants might feel compelled to accept exploitative working conditions or multiple jobs, jeopardising their physical and mental well-being in their pursuit of financial stability.

While employers impose rigorous standards on migrants, these individuals, particularly women, are often bound by familial obligations and a shortage of domestic support. Family ties exert an overwhelming influence, hindering independent decision-making and career advancement. The expectations of partners, parents, in-laws, and extended family members often clash with professional aspirations, stifling motivation. Trapped in low-level positions within developed nations, many migrants experience deteriorating mental health as they compare their circumstances to the successes of former classmates in their home countries. Moreover, certain migrant visa categories may limit their options for career progression or entrepreneurship, further exacerbating their financial strain. The lack of recognition for overseas qualifications and experience can also force highly skilled migrants into low-paying, menial jobs, adding to their frustration and sense of unfulfilled potential.

I previously held the misconception that a master's degree was the sole pathway to career advancement, so I invested significant time and money in pursuing this qualification. The Australian Bureau of Statistics and Diversity Council Australia confirmed that many migrants feel they're 'overqualified and underutilised' in their jobs, leading to a stagnation in their career development. These statistics underline the systemic challenges that migrants face in achieving upward mobility in the Australian workforce. However, I've come to realise that a degree is just one tool in the career advancement toolbox. Other equally effective strategies can propel your career forward in the corporate world, often at a fraction of the cost and time commitment. I encourage all the migrants who want to change roles to quickly invest their time in different effective alternatives like:

1. Identify the current trends and needs of the corporate world and pursue the necessary certifications with any online educational opportunities available.
2. Spend time networking with professionals to identify their valuable insights and connections.
3. Volunteering for high-visibility projects or initiatives at work is a great way to be seen and position yourself for future promotions or leadership roles.
4. Seek out internal mobility opportunities, lateral moves, or job rotations within your current organisation. New challenges always help you broaden your skillset and increase your visibility to senior leadership.
5. Building a strong personal brand by cultivating a positive online presence and actively contributing to your field through community involvement is a great way to establish yourself as an expert and attract potential employers or collaborators.

Learning from the stories of other successful leaders and their paths to success can be a great source of inspiration, highlighting the diverse routes one can take to achieve their goals. Since career advancement is a multifaceted journey, a combination of efforts and thoughts connected with your individual goals and circumstances always help unlock your full potential and achieve success in the corporate world.

I was surrounded by experienced and expert people in the same industry, yet I failed to actively seek their insights or advice on career growth and progression. Reflecting on this, I realise that my own biased thoughts hindered me from seeking help or openly discussing challenges at work. It was a combination of a conscious fear of being judged for my skillset and an unconscious worry about potential backstabbing that prevented me from reaching out. My error in confining my network to familiar cultural and social circles further limited my opportunities for growth and diverse perspectives. As a consequence of the family violence I endured, I found myself isolated from my community and deprived of valuable opportunities for growth and learning within my own cultural context. The separation severed those vital connections, leaving me feeling adrift and disconnected. Consequently, I had to navigate the complexities of career advancement, mental health struggles, and societal pressures entirely on my own, all while maintaining a facade of strength and resilience in my professional life.

In certain cultures, there exists a powerful norm, often intertwined with religious beliefs, where individuals forge strong connections and offer support within their own communities. This sense of shared identity and faith fosters a deep-rooted bond and a willingness to assist one another in various aspects of life, including career advancement. The migrant community I belong to comprises a mix of clinicians and IT professionals, many of whom prioritise financial stability and view their careers primarily as a source of income. This mindset often leads them to pursue entrepreneurial ventures alongside their partners rather than focusing solely on climbing the corporate ladder. This prevalent mindset within the migrant community can inadvertently contribute to the perpetuation of biased mindsets within their corporate workplaces.

The lack of ambition for traditional career advancement among some migrant professionals might be misconstrued as a lack of drive or commitment, potentially reinforcing stereotypes and hindering their opportunities for growth and recognition. Additionally, the focus on external business ventures could be perceived as a divided loyalty, further marginalising them within the corporate environment. This creates a complex dynamic where the cultural and professional aspirations of certain migrant groups might clash with the expectations and norms of the dominant corporate culture. This disconnect can lead to misunderstandings, missed opportunities, and the reinforcement of unconscious biases, ultimately impeding their career progression and contributing to a less inclusive workplace.

Inspired

I've personally witnessed the impact of generational mindsets within my own community. The pressure to follow in previous generations' footsteps, pursue specific careers, or adhere to traditional values can be stifling. While these expectations often stem from a place of love and a desire for success, they can inadvertently limit individual potential and perpetuate outdated norms. I believe it's crucial for us to break free from these constraints and embrace a mindset of growth and exploration. We should strive to reach beyond the familiar, challenge societal expectations, and forge our own unique paths. By leaving behind generational mindsets, we open ourselves up to a world of possibilities and empower future generations to do the same. It's time to redefine success on our own terms and embrace the full spectrum of human potential.

Nevertheless, there are now proven methods and examples of migrants ascending to the highest levels of various industries. I acknowledge the outstanding achievements of migrants like Vik Bansal, Preeti Bajaj, Dr. Munjed Al Muderis, Tan Le, Aminata Conteh-Biger, Dr. Munjed Al Muderis, Sam Bashiry, Ravi Bhatia, Raj Nair, Amitabh Mattoo, Shemara Wikramanayake, Roy Singh, Manuri Gunawardena, Le Ho, and Nasra Aden. Their journeys, though inspiring, were fraught with obstacles that they overcame through determination, dedication, and mentorship. As Australia's dependence on skilled Indian workers grows, we can anticipate an increase in similar success stories as challenges are gradually eradicated.

But why do the normal migrants not have a success story in their corporate ladder, or are they comfortable with the work-life balance style of their career and connecting more to the community? It took me years to discover the wealth of free resources and courses within our organisations. I've realised we must identify targeted support programs, mentorship, and bridging courses to empower us migrants to conquer challenges and ascend to leadership positions. Yet, the harsh truth is that many of us remain stagnant in our roles for prolonged periods. Observing the homogenous composition of board members across

Conscious and Unconscious Bias: Mitigating Workplace Inequalities

the country and core members in many different organisations, my motivation to uncover more success stories is fading. Is there a rise in biased leadership within corporate structures?

Our personal histories unconsciously shape our biases towards race, religion, gender, ability, or age. Children as young as three internalise these biases from their parents. I was shocked to discover my own unconscious biases inherited from my family. Recognising that the ingrained desire to please others and initiate group conversations stems from my mother's influence, highlighting the powerful impact of familial biases. My exploration of the family's history and connection to the bias is helping me connect with the core of our generations. Uncovering the generational transmission of biases through conversations with my mother is a piece of powerful evidence of the complex interplay of nature and nurture. It's inspiring to see that commitment to conscious rewiring and dedication to peeling back the layers of our complexities will showcase great changes in our thoughts and actions. This is where the beginning of change happens in all areas of life, and even your close contacts cannot understand the authenticity of your conversion.

Uncovering these deeply rooted patterns was a pivotal step in my personal growth. Overcoming these deeply ingrained perspectives requires deliberate effort and a commitment to personal growth. While challenging, the journey towards a more inclusive mindset is undeniably worthwhile. We need to remember the truth that every person has a bias—both conscious and unconscious. We have strategies to deal with the biases we know about, but it's hard to deal with unconscious bias if we're not practicing mindfulness. Acknowledging our own feelings and other people's feelings about our actions and words, assessing the situations, understanding the accusations and the wrong part we played, and modifying those in our future are the best ways to reduce our unconscious bias.

While the Blue Eyes and Brown Eyes Experiment is widely condemned for its unethical treatment of children, it unquestionably highlighted the profound impact of bias on young minds. I believe similar discriminatory practices persist within corporate environments and, at different times, became the victim for these discriminations.

A colleague, previously a vocal advocate for social causes in their home country, had transformed into a remarkably quiet presence within our workplace. Open conversations about workplace bias revealed that self-doubt had hindered their professional progression. Surprisingly, this individual recently secured a deputy C-level role, the sole Asian representative within the leadership team. Their journey is a testament to the power of supportive leadership, as their mentor actively championed their advancement, disregarding prevalent biases. Such instances of equitable leadership are commendable but, unfortunately, remain exceptional in the corporate landscape.

Migrants from non-Asian backgrounds often exhibit a strong sense of self-worth, enabling them to navigate challenges with resilience. For example, a Greek friend, now an Australian resident, expressed unwavering confidence in her abilities, unfazed by limited recognition or career advancement opportunities in her workplace. Prioritising work-life balance and personal fulfillment over rapid career progression, she exemplified a healthier approach to her professional life. While influenced by financial needs and career aspirations, this mindset underscores the importance of self-value and commitment to maintaining peace of mind in today's competitive landscape. She's a positive role model for Asian migrants who often grapple with feelings of missed opportunities in corporate environments.

Diversity Australia has identified three prevalent types of biases at work: Affinity Bias, Social Comparison Bias, and Confirmatory Bias. Unfortunately, exploring the current culture of diversity reveals numerous instances of unconscious bias occurring in workplaces, often accepted as 'normal' or simply part of the organisational fabric.

Conscious and Unconscious Bias: Mitigating Workplace Inequalities

This normalisation of bias is a significant obstacle to creating truly inclusive and equitable workplaces. It allows discriminatory practices to persist, hindering the progress of individuals from marginalised groups and perpetuating systemic inequalities. To combat this, we must actively challenge the notion that bias is 'normal.' We need to cultivate awareness, educate ourselves and others about the various forms of unconscious bias, and hold ourselves and our organisations accountable for creating environments where everyone feels valued, respected, and empowered to thrive. Only then can we break down these deeply ingrained biases and create a workplace culture that celebrates diversity and fosters true inclusion.

Unless your organisation or leaders acknowledge these biases, they cannot take action to address them in the workplace. The responsibility, then, falls on each of us who experience inequality. We must find our voice, speak up, and firmly believe these injustices are unacceptable. Don't let fear or doubt silence you; your courage can spark change and pave the way for a more inclusive and equitable future for everyone.

To cultivate a motivated and engaged workforce, organisations should strive to implement promotion processes that are both unbiased and transparent. This ensures that employees feel valued and recognised for their contributions while fostering a sense of fairness and equal opportunity within the workplace. Organisations can implement different strategies like internal job postings readily available to all employees, encouraging them to explore opportunities for advancement within the organisation, offering opportunities for lateral moves or job rotations that allow employees to gain experience in different areas, and actively promoting diversity and inclusion in the workplace to ensure that promotion processes are fair and equitable for all employees, regardless of their background or identity, to facilitate career advancement and provide opportunities for employees to 'jump the ladder.' By adopting these strategies, organisations can create a culture of transparency, fairness, and opportunity, empowering employees to take ownership of their career development and achieve their full potential. This, in turn, leads to a more engaged, motivated, and productive workforce, benefiting both individuals and the organisation as a whole.

Daily Reflection for Migrants to Workplace Inequalities:

1. Self-Awareness and Values: Do I regularly take time to reflect on my values, attitudes, and work practices, especially considering how they might interact with those of others in my workplace?
2. Fairness and Equality: Am I treating all my stakeholders and peers equally, providing the same level of service and attention, regardless of their background or cultural differences?
3. Cultural Sensitivity: Am I mindful of cultural factors when interacting with stakeholders, and do I actively challenge any prejudices or stereotypes that might arise?
4. Taking Responsibility: If someone feels disconnected or rejected, do I acknowledge my role in that, or do I dismiss it as solely their problem?
5. Equal Opportunities: Am I actively ensuring that everyone has access to the same opportunities, regardless of their cultural background or identity?
6. Open Communication: Have I established clear and accessible channels for communication, enabling everyone to provide feedback and share their perspectives?
7. Inclusive Social Activities: Am I supporting and participating in social activities that are welcoming and inclusive to everyone in the workplace?
8. Acknowledging Diversity: Am I recognising and celebrating diverse cultural and religious holidays and events?

Conscious and Unconscious Bias: Mitigating Workplace Inequalities

9. Respectful Language: Am I using inclusive language that doesn't make assumptions about sexual orientation or gender identity?
10. Accommodating Religious Needs: Am I making reasonable accommodations for religious practices, such as prayer times, dietary restrictions, and clothing requirements?
11. Unconscious Bias: Am I aware of any unconscious biases I might have and how they might affect my interactions with others? Am I putting in extra effort to communicate effectively with those culturally different from me?
12. Cross-Cultural Interaction: How effectively do I interact with colleagues at all levels who come from different cultural backgrounds?

These questions are meant to encourage ongoing self-reflection and growth to avoid unconscious biased decision-making and thought processes in our workplace. By consistently examining our own biases and actions, we can strive to create a more inclusive and welcoming environment for everyone.

Chapter 4

Cultivating Commitment: *Igniting Your Inner Fire*

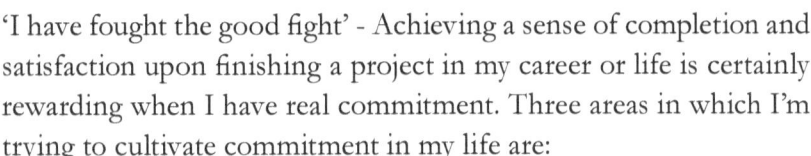

'I have fought the good fight' - Achieving a sense of completion and satisfaction upon finishing a project in my career or life is certainly rewarding when I have real commitment. Three areas in which I'm trying to cultivate commitment in my life are:

- Commitment to my core and self
- Commitment to community and family
- Commitment to my career and workplace

Everyone who commits to themselves feels the truth that there's no such thing as balancing work and family. It's a constant juggling act. And many times, the people in our lives, our immediate circle, are the real supporters or demotivators. I love being a raw—real, authentic, and worthy—mom, chilling and chatting with my boys, and discovering cool new stuff together. From dreaming up crazy ideas, idioms, movies, and videos to binge-watching funny shows, we're always on an adventure in our own space. I love whipping up delicious meals and getting them excited about food. I enjoy being real and love losing myself in their *Minecraft* world, building my dream home from scratch. It's like creating a whole new universe where I'm the ultimate designer, even if I have no clue about mining. A deep sense of peace washes over me as I watch my boys grow, learning about our faith and sharing the core values of our family: love, joy, and peace.

Exploring nature with them is like recharging my soul, and hanging out with friends is my happy place, where we share everything from heartbreaks to hilarious moments. Every night, I count down the minutes until I hear my mom's voice. It's like connecting with three generations in one call. I used to love watching her try to teach my kids our mother tougue. It was hilarious and heart-warming at the same time. But the absence of my father, a hero etched in my heart, is a wound that time softens but never fully heals. I treasure every moment with my family. Again, the ache of missing out on special times and losing touch with people I care about is a heavy weight to carry. These experiences have tempered my soul, forging a resilience that forces me forward.

It's a common challenge to reconcile our personal goals with the demands and sacrifices of family life. The pain of missed opportunities can be overwhelming, especially when coupled with a strong sense of purpose. But in my life, I had to redefine my success and purpose within my family. In those days, I did similar personal development tasks that all others tried in different ways. I learned about setting clear boundaries at a very late stage of my life. Prioritising my well-being, finding outlets to recharge myself, finding meaning in loss, understanding how past experiences have shaped me, and using pain as power and motivation to live a more fulfilling life by focusing on the present are the major areas I modified in my personal life with commitment.

Cultivating Commitment: Igniting Your Inner Fire

I constantly had to remind myself and tell my brain that it's okay to feel overwhelmed or conflicted. This is a journey, and there's no perfect solution. The key is to find what works best for me and my family. We focused on building new experiences and traditions and started to take life as seasons with full commitment but not a lifelong commitment. Discovering my true self is a journey into the unknown. I've learned that taking charge of my life, with clear goals and a strong will, means accepting the results, good or bad. It's been a tough road, but it's lit a fire inside me. I still have a long way to go. I'm learning that true strength lies not in avoiding challenges but in embracing them with commitment.

Reflecting inward, I realise that my values have shifted, and with them, so should my commitments. I once clung to the belief that lifelong dedication was a moral imperative, even when it extinguished my internal fire. Now, I understand that true commitment isn't about endurance but alignment. By honouring my evolving self, I'm reclaiming my energy to pursue a path filled with purpose and passion. This journey, though uncertain, is far more fulfilling than a life lived in stagnant obligation.

We need practise for our body and mind to commit. The power of inner stillness is needed for the commitment. Emotion and intention are clearly related and need to modify our body with our intake to the body and mind. The commitment is related to the body stages; we're punished by the attitudes we have and the intake we do for our bodies and minds.

Setting achievable goals and consistently following through was crucial for building my commitment. I committed to earning one industry certification annually to fuel my professional growth. Additionally, I actively sought opportunities to join group activities, ensuring consistent engagement within the community. These incremental steps proved instrumental in maintaining motivation and propelling my career forward. At the same time, I realised that commitment is a two-way street. It requires dedication from both the individual and the organisation.

I recall a friend who embarked on her Australian journey as a volunteer. With her technical expertise, she immersed herself in learning new programming languages. Her unwavering dedication transformed her into a skilled professional, ultimately securing a permanent role within the company.

I work in a high-pressure environment at one of Melbourne's major trauma hospitals. Being a backend IT professional, my typical workday used to extend well beyond traditional hours, and the concept of remote work or a hybrid work model was entirely foreign. Before the pandemic, intellectual intelligence was the primary metric for career success. The prevailing notion was that high IQ equated to high-paying jobs and fulfilling lifestyles. However, the COVID-19 crisis ushered in a new era marked by a heightened emphasis on mental health, work-life balance, equity, diversity, and inclusion. A blessing in disguise for many professionals, including us.

While comfort can be a pleasant feeling, it often indicates a lack of challenge and growth. To foster a more fulfilling and rewarding work experience, it's essential to step out of your comfort zone and embrace new challenges. I made a conscious effort to step outside my comfort zone and take on new challenges. I sought out opportunities to learn new skills, build relationships, and contribute to the organisation in meaningful ways. By proactively seeking out new experiences and stepping outside my comfort zone, I was able to broaden my horizons and grow both personally and professionally. It was not an immediate growth; it was a consistent and patient way of cultivating my commitment style.

Cultivating Commitment: Igniting Your Inner Fire

What did I do to make changes in my commitment style?

Strategy	Explanation	Benefits
Ask for Help	Don't hesitate to seek assistance from colleagues, friends, or family when needed.	Reduces stress, improves efficiency, and fosters stronger relationships.
Show Loyalty and Dedication	Demonstrate your commitment to your work and the organisation.	Builds trust and respect with your colleagues and superiors.
Collaborate Effectively	Work well with others to achieve shared goals.	Improves teamwork, productivity, and problem-solving.
Balance Your Life	Prioritise different areas of your life, such as work, family, and personal interests.	Reduces stress, improves overall well-being, and prevents burnout.
Pursue Your Passion	Engage in activities that you enjoy and find fulfilling.	Increases motivation, creativity, and job satisfaction.
Embrace Challenges	View challenges as opportunities for growth and learning.	Builds resilience and adaptability.
Create a Vision Board	Visualise your goals and aspirations to stay motivated and focused.	Provides a clear roadmap for your future and helps you stay on track.

When I had to leave everything behind after 18 years of family life for a core reason, I had to start again with three little children. The commitment I made to raise a better family by spreading the message of the power of respecting women was an apt but tough decision.

Inspired

I wanted them to understand the need to help others, show some kindness, love, and joy, and spread that peace around the world. As a single mother, my unwavering commitment to my children has been my guiding force. I've strived to provide them with a safe, loving, and nurturing environment, free from violence and fear. The journey has been challenging, filled with moments of doubt and uncertainty. But I've persevered, driven by my love for my children and my determination to create a better future for them.

I've learned that providing for my children's basic needs is essential, but it's equally important to nurture their emotional and psychological well-being. I've faced countless obstacles, from financial struggles to the emotional turmoil of single parenthood but I've never wavered in my commitment to my children. My love for my children is my greatest source of inspiration. It fuels my determination to overcome challenges, provide for their needs, and create a brighter future for them.

My journey of spiritual and personal growth has been a transformative experience. I'm committed to cultivating a deeper connection with myself and the world around me. I believe that by nurturing my spiritual well-being, I can unlock my full potential and live a more fulfilling life. I have placed my good faith in that, taking my children along the way. This fire helped me find out my soul's spiritual purpose and connect with that inner fire. My commitment to spiritual growth is an ongoing journey, and I'm excited to see where it will lead me.

Cultivating Your Inner Fire is a Journey of 3 Ps - Purpose, Process, and Payoff. I learned ways to utilise these from different studies and researchers that I pursued.

Purpose:

- Identify your passions: What truly excites and motivates you? What are you naturally drawn to?

- Align your values: Ensure your goals and aspirations align with your core values.
- Define your mission: Clearly articulate your purpose and what you want to achieve.

Process:

- Set SMART goals: Establish specific, measurable, achievable, relevant, and time-bound goals.
- Create a plan: Develop a roadmap to guide your journey towards your goals.
- Take action: Start small and gradually build momentum. Celebrate your achievements along the way.
- Learn from setbacks: View challenges as opportunities for growth and learning.
- Seek support: Surround yourself with positive and supportive people who believe in you.

Payoff:

- Increased motivation: A strong sense of purpose can fuel your motivation and drive.
- Enhanced well-being: Pursuing meaningful goals can contribute to greater happiness and fulfillment.
- Positive impact: Making a difference in the world can provide a deep sense of satisfaction and purpose.
- Personal growth: Overcoming challenges and achieving your goals can lead to significant personal growth and development.

Inspired

With this exercise, I identified that I need to learn more about the Wheel of Life. It's an extremely powerful tool that helped me align my commitment. The different areas I'm sowing seeds of commitment in my life are:

Areas of life	Strategies	Benefits
Wealth	Financial planning, investment, debt management	Financial security, peace of mind
Health	Regular check-ups, healthy lifestyle, stress management	Physical and mental well-being, longevity
Family	Quality time, open communication, support	Strong relationships, emotional fulfillment
Fun	Hobbies, social connections, experiences	Joy, relaxation, personal fulfillment
Wellness	Mental health, self-care, mindfulness	Overall well-being, stress reduction
Community	Volunteering, networking, civic engagement	Social connection, giving back
Career	Goal setting, professional development, networking	Job satisfaction, career advancement
Studies	Time management, seeking support, organisation	Academic success, personal growth
Spirituality	Regular practice, open-mindedness, self-reflection	Inner peace, purpose, connection

Cultivating Commitment: Igniting Your Inner Fire

I've made another commitment with PowerTalk. It's a communication technique that involves using positive affirmations and visualisations to enhance motivation and commitment. By focusing on positive outcomes and using empowering language, individuals can strengthen their belief in themselves and their abilities. I learned these from mentors who have helped me improve my commitment on a daily basis. And yes, it works!

How PowerTalk Works

1. Identify your goals: Clearly define what you want to achieve over a period of time.
2. Use positive affirmations: Repeat positive statements about yourself and your abilities. For example, 'I am becoming a leader in one year because I'm capable of achieving my goal.'
3. Visualise success: Create a mental image of yourself achieving your goals. Vision boards are good tools to remind you of the success you're working towards.
4. Practise self-talk: Say it out loud to yourself on a daily basis so your brain starts to believe it. Write a script and say it out loud as your first words of the day. Record it and make sure not to skip it.
5. Take action: Believe in yourself and take the necessary steps to achieve your goals.

Benefits of PowerTalk

- Increased motivation: Positive affirmations can boost your motivation and drive.
- Improved self-confidence: Believing in yourself can help you overcome challenges and setbacks.
- Enhanced focus: Visualisation can help you stay focused on your goals and avoid distractions.
- Reduced stress: Positive self-talk can help reduce stress and anxiety.

- Greater resilience: PowerTalk can help you develop resilience and bounce back from setbacks.

It's scientifically proven that positive self-talk can rewire the brain, boosting our confidence and helping us achieve our goals. If you're looking for a starting point, I found success with this simple approach: The power of commitment to the three Cs.

Commitment to Core and Self:

- Self-discovery: Embark on a journey of self-discovery to gain deeper insights into your strengths, weaknesses, values, and passions.
- Self-direction: Chart your course by setting clear, achievable goals that align with your purpose and values.
- Self-improvement: Cultivate a mindset of continuous learning and development, seeking opportunities to expand your knowledge and skills.
- Self-nurturing: Prioritise self-care by making time for activities that nourish your physical, mental, and emotional well-being.
- Self-empowerment: Develop the resilience and inner strength to bounce back from setbacks, embrace challenges, and persevere in the face of adversity.

Commitment to Community and family:

- Cherished Moments: Prioritise quality time with loved ones and nurture meaningful relationships.
- Compassionate Support: Offer unwavering support and encouragement to your family members and friends, fostering a sense of belonging and connection.
- Community Engagement: Actively participate in community activities and initiatives, contributing to the well-being of your local area and fostering a sense of shared responsibility.

- Cultural Bridge-Building: Foster meaningful connections between different cultures and generations, celebrating diversity and promoting understanding.

Commitment to Career and Workplace:

- Professional Growth: Actively seek out opportunities for learning and development to enhance your skills and expertise in your career.
- Professional Fulfillment: Strive to maintain a healthy balance between your professional responsibilities and personal life, prioritising your well-being and overall happiness.
- Professional Connections: Cultivate meaningful relationships with colleagues and industry professionals, expanding your network and fostering valuable connections.
- Professional Leadership: Embrace opportunities to take on leadership roles, inspire others, and share your knowledge and expertise as a mentor
- Professional Contribution: Dedicate yourself to giving back to your organisation, actively contributing to its success, and making a positive impact on your team and colleagues.

While striving for personal fulfillment, I once felt discouraged, believing my dream version of success was unattainable, rendering my commitments meaningless. I mistakenly held the limiting belief that if someone else had already achieved my desired outcome, it was no longer an option for me. But upon realising that happiness and success are boundless and each person's journey is unique, I recommitted myself to my dreams, this time with a newfound sense of freedom and possibility.

This commitment to self-worth and personal boundaries is intrinsically linked to the concept I explored in another chapter. When we truly value ourselves and establish healthy boundaries, we invite others to interact with us on those same terms, fostering relationships built on mutual respect and understanding. It's crucial to give the people in our lives the space they need to contribute to and support our dreams. This doesn't mean relinquishing control or relying solely on others; it's about striking a balance between self-reliance and openness to collaboration. Actively seek out and listen to the advice of those who genuinely care about your success while ultimately taking ownership of your decisions and dreams. By embracing this approach, we empower ourselves to overcome challenges and achieve our aspirations without falling into the trap of victimhood or saviour complexes. Remember, true success is a collaborative journey fuelled by self-belief, commitment, healthy boundaries, and a willingness to learn and grow alongside those who champion our dreams.

My soul-searching journey led me to explore the vast realm of spirituality, which inspired me to start a radio show to share my insights. I firmly believe that spirituality isn't exclusive to the highly religious. I've encountered countless individuals who radiate a spirit of love, joy, and peace, drawing inspiration from various faiths and belief systems. However, some friends perceived my spiritual exploration as a departure from my own faith, prompting a profound awakening and a re-evaluation of societal expectations. This experience highlighted how the corporate world often inadvertently stifles spirituality.

Yet, history abounds with examples of individuals who harnessed their spiritual connection to achieve extraordinary feats, even within challenging environments. Mother Teresa's unwavering devotion to serving the poorest of the poor, fuelled by her deep Catholic faith, transformed countless lives and inspired a global movement of compassion. Oprah Winfrey, driven by her belief in personal empowerment and spiritual growth, built a media empire that touched millions, fostering a sense of connection and purpose in her audience. Furthermore, many individuals excelling in the corporate world attribute their success, in part, to a strong connection to their spirituality.

Numerous examples showcase how various spiritual practices have positively impacted individuals within the corporate world and beyond. Sri Sri Ravi Shankar's Art of Living Foundation, through its emphasis on mindfulness and meditation, has helped countless professionals manage stress, improve focus, and enhance overall well-being, ultimately leading to increased productivity and job satisfaction.

The Sikh community's selfless service through initiatives like the langar (free community kitchen) exemplifies the power of compassion and generosity, qualities that resonate deeply within the corporate world and foster a sense of social responsibility.

The Buddhist and Islamic communities, with their emphasis on mindfulness, ethical conduct, and compassion, have also cultivated leaders who excel in the corporate sphere. The Islamic practice of Zakat (obligatory charity) and Sadaqah (voluntary charity) encourages giving back to the community and supporting those in need. This emphasis on social responsibility can inspire corporate social responsibility initiatives and encourage businesses to make a positive impact on society. These demonstrate that a strong spiritual foundation can serve as a powerful compass, guiding them towards ethical decision-making, empathy, and a genuine desire to create positive change within their organisations and communities. In its various manifestations, spirituality is not incompatible with success in the corporate world. In fact, it can be a powerful catalyst for personal and professional growth, fostering qualities that are essential for effective leadership and sustainable business practices. By embracing spirituality in the workplace, individuals and organisations alike can unlock their full potential and contribute to a more compassionate and fulfilling world.

Throughout this chapter, we've explored the multifaceted nature of commitment, its profound impact on our personal and professional lives, and its transformative power in shaping our destinies. We've delved into the complexities of setting boundaries, navigating societal expectations, and embracing our unique paths to success. Ultimately, the journey of commitment is an ongoing process of self-discovery, growth, and resilience. It requires us to nurture our inner fire to cultivate a deep connection to our core values and purpose. It calls us to challenge limiting beliefs, embrace vulnerability, and step boldly into the unknown. As we navigate the complexities of life and the ever-evolving landscape of the corporate world, let us remember that true fulfillment lies in aligning our actions with our deepest aspirations. By embracing commitment in all its forms, we unlock our boundless potential and embark on a lifelong learning, growth, and impact journey.

The relentless pursuit of productivity and profit can overshadow the importance of inner connection and purpose. In such an environment, losing sight of our core values and the deeper meaning behind our work is easy. I believe that true connection to our core, our spirit, is essential for fulfilling our purpose, both personally and professionally. When we live in alignment with our values, we tap into a wellspring of inspiration and motivation that propels us forward, even in the face of adversity. So, let us ignite our inner fire, cultivate unwavering commitment, and embrace the transformative power of living a purpose-driven life. The journey may be challenging, at the same time **inspring**, but the rewards are immeasurable.

Chapter 5

Conquer Your Fear: *Championing Confidence*

My childhood self was a fearless explorer, unafraid of the unknown. I vividly recall walking alone to the clinic for injections, an almost unimaginable level of independence, earning me a reputation of unwavering confidence. I was a hero for many in our little community, and I had to keep that level of confidence until I was alone in my life. It's perplexing to look back and wonder when this fearless spirit began to fade. The illusion shattered when I found myself alone, revealing a trembling core of fear, shame, and anxiety. I slowly realised that it wasn't real confidence that we need in life. Unexpected journeys in life and work have helped me identify the intensity of my own confidence, which forced me to seek ways to conquer my fear.

It astounded me to discover that humans are inherently wired with only two primal fears: falling and loud noises. This revelation came to me late in life after four decades of handling a multitude of anxieties. I had erroneously assumed that my fears were universal, particularly those that emerged after immigrating to a new country. Over the past quarter-century, I had constructed a facade of boldness and confidence, a carefully crafted image that masked my inner turmoil. The irony is that those closest to me perceived only this outward appearance, oblivious to the trembling foundation upon which it was built. Their inability to comprehend my journey towards self-discovery was a constant source of frustration. Yet, I was determined to dismantle the fortress of fear that had imprisoned me for so long. By conquering these shadows, I believed I could rediscover the authentic self that once existed. Freedom from fear is the key to unlocking a life filled with joy and purpose. The ultimate aspiration is to attain a state of profound peace, a serenity that will allow me to sleep soundly without the weight of anxiety.

I always feel that rather than being shaped by my experiences, my brain keeps them as a repository. It's a vast archive, storing every sensation, thought, and emotion. The danger lies in becoming so engrossed in these collected experiences that we lose sight of the present. It's as if the mind becomes a prisoner of its own past, unable to break free and engage fully with the world.

The sheer terror I felt when one cockroach crawled over me is a memory etched into my soul. With courage that astounded me, my father calmly picked up the live cockroach. With patience and wisdom, he dissected my fear. He explained their habits, harmless nature, and crucial role in the ecosystem. Gradually, the monster transformed into a misunderstood creature. Empowered by newfound knowledge, I conquered my fear. The thrill of overcoming my terror was exhilarating. I went from being a petrified child to a cockroach wrangler, much to the dismay of my unsuspecting brothers holding its long antennas and calling 'pata' (the Malayalam word for cockroach).

Years later, as a parent myself, I found my children mirroring my childhood terror. The same fear I once knew gripped their tiny bodies. Remembering my father's wisdom, I decided to be their hero.

Conquer Your Fear: Championing Confidence

I gently introduced them to the world of cockroaches, explaining their role in nature and dispelling the myths. Watching their fear slowly transform into curiosity was one of the most rewarding experiences of my life. Just as my father had done for me, I had passed on the torch of courage and understanding to the next generation.

My childhood was a mix of lush green paddy fields and the sounds of the countryside. Paddy fields stretched out as far as the eye could see, a verdant expanse teeming with life. It was in this idyllic setting that I first encountered the creatures that would forever etch themselves into my memory: snakes. Initially, these stories were mere whispers, distant threats that failed to chill my young blood. But then came the day when reality shattered the illusion of safety. News of tragic deaths caused by venomous bites in neighbouring houses sent shockwaves through my mind. Though I tried to be brave, the chilling narratives seeped into my young mind, casting a long shadow over my innocent world. Even today, the mere image of a snake triggers a primal response, a fight-or-flight instinct that overrides reason. It's as though my childhood brain has been permanently etched with the image of danger, and every encounter with a snake is a painful reminder of that fear. It's ironic that this creature, often worshipped as a symbol of power and wisdom in many belief systems, has been transformed into a harbinger of terror in my mind. While cultures around the world have revered it, I've been conditioned by my religious perspective to associate it with sin, death, and evil. This clash of cultural interpretations has created a deep-seated fear that continues to shape my perception.

The reality of having zero savings after a lengthy 18 years in a corporate career, coupled with a sudden separation, was emotionally devastating. Transforming into a single parent with the sole responsibility of caring for three young sons in a day was a daunting experience. 'Was that an act of confidence or survival?' I used to ask that many times while prioritising our basic needs. Transforming a bare townhouse into a home using second-hand finds was not my dream of confidence. A toxic mix of anger, shame, self-doubt, anxiety, and the mental anguish of legal proceedings, coupled with frequent family health crises, eroded my confidence and physical well-being. The relentless demands of corporate life persisted amidst this turmoil. Fear of jeopardising employment prevented me from disclosing these challenges to my employers. A subsequent cerebral aneurysm diagnosis demanded unwavering strength, forcing me to suppress my vulnerabilities. While externally presenting a facade of resilience, internally, I grappled with a profound sense of obligation to my only supportive family in the community. But I was learning that unexpected journeys in life and the corporate world will help you build confidence.

As a foreign-born individual, the pressure to express myself fluently with local slang was massive. Simple tasks like placing a McDonald's drive-thru order became a daunting ordeal. Juggling three children's diverse preferences, I often found myself hesitant to explain the combinations of sauces and sizes in the right way. The inevitable need for clarification at the next window was humiliating, compounded by my children's visible disappointment. Over time, this experience eroded my confidence in ordering food, forcing me to meticulously script orders or delegate the task to my teenagers. The root of my anxiety lay in the fear of linguistic inadequacy and the shame associated with miscommunication during the ordering process. When I realised that confidence isn't a static state but a dynamic process shaped by experiences and through personal growth, I evolved, ready to get help to articulate these orders in a better way. I'm eager to hear from other parents who might have experienced similar language-related challenges with their teenage children. While research indicates that bilingualism enhances cognitive function, my personal experiences reveal the challenges of mental translation. The potential benefits of delayed cognitive decline are encouraging research, but the daily effort to switch between languages can be taxing.

Our present-day beliefs are a direct consequence of our childhood experiences, shaped by parental attitudes and even influenced by our mother's emotional state during pregnancy. Despite exposure to concepts of inner healing and the link between parenting and childhood trauma within Christian teachings, I dismissed the notion that maternal emotions could be transmitted to offspring. It wasn't until I embarked on a personal journey of self-discovery, guided by a mentor, that I began to question my deeply ingrained beliefs. My father was my unwavering hero, a towering figure who cast a long shadow. I believed wholeheartedly that my strengths, character, and everything I was stemmed directly from him. However, as the years unfolded, with my conscious reflection on my fears and lack of confidence, a shaking realisation emerged: the shadows that lurked within me, the fears and insecurities that had subtly shaped my life, held origins beyond my father's influence. I confess to a distant relationship with my mother for many years. It wasn't until his passing that I embarked on a journey of self-discovery, a path that unexpectedly led me closer to my mother.

Through open and honest conversations with my mother, a new and powerful connection between our thoughts and feelings emerged. I discovered a hidden depth to my mother. The woman I once knew as a quiet people pleaser was, in fact, a vibrant young woman brimming with confidence. The constraints of marriage and motherhood had seemingly muffled her spirit. Yet, in the quiet strength she exuded, I found a profound respect and admiration. Her resilience, hidden beneath layers of self-sacrifice, is a testament to the extraordinary woman she is. But, I discovered that the emotional confusion she endured during pregnancy had a great impression on my life.

My journey towards conquering fear started in 2014, initially marked by superficial coping mechanisms. However, a profound shift occurred in late 2021 when I recognised the inauthenticity of my confidence. Driven by a desire to understand my underlying fears, I immersed myself in different resources available in the market. This introspection revealed a disconnect between my spiritual practices and genuine faith. By reconnecting with my core values, I laid the foundation to experience the true meaning of spirituality. This was my stepping stone.

Inspired

Rather than dwelling on the past and assigning blame, we must cultivate forgiveness and understanding. By releasing the grip of the past, we can break free from the chains of old patterns and create a brighter future for ourselves and generations to come. It's about finding peace within ourselves, not perpetuating cycles of blame and resentment. I believe my experiences are far from unique, and many others must be navigating similar challenges and emotions. By breaking the silence surrounding these often-hidden experiences, I hope to offer comfort and support to those facing similar challenges.

This realisation marked the beginning of my true transformative journey towards self-confidence. As I delved deeper into the roots of my insecurities, I discovered how the emotional climate of my childhood had shaped my perception of myself and the world. By understanding the origins of my fears and limitations, I was able to challenge them, gradually building a stronger sense of self-worth. This confidence has empowered me to break free from the patterns of the past and embrace a brighter future.

I committed myself to the core connection with my Creator and spirituality, which gave me the confidence to face my life, eradicate my fears with clear affirmations, and retrain my brain. Empowered by a deepened spiritual connection, I embarked on a series of learning experiences. This confidence inspired me to launch an English-language show on our community radio station, a contrast to my previously limited communication skills. Reflecting on my linguistic struggles in 2000, this endeavour seemed a brave action for me. My children became my initial audience, and their support fostered the courage to share my show with a wider community. Gradually, I expanded my reach, sharing the venture with community members. The overwhelming support and encouragement fuelled my growth, transforming me from a hesitant speaker to a confident communicator. Within two years, I hosted over 500 segments, and more than 150 guests participated, creating valuable connections and accelerating my community services. I was experiencing this verse in my life: 'When an intelligent person hears a wise saying, he praises it and adds to it.'

I continued to fill myself with different studies, life stories, podcasts, and people around me. Many different people gave me inspiration, guidance, learnings, and confidence tips in my recent corporate and community life. Indra Nooyi, an Indian-born American businesswoman, the first woman of colour, and the first immigrant to head a Fortune 50 company, was a great inspiration for many leaders. I was inspired by her confidence and strategies in boosting confidence. I started to practise what she used to share, 'Even if we don't have much to say, we need to say it with more confidence, not softer.' We need to sit up and share our great values with much confidence in order to be heard in this corporate world. The inner strength to tackle challenges and display self-assurance in every situation is the new way I modelled myself to showcase my confidence.

While life often presents unexpected storms, for me, it was a tempestuous blend of domestic turmoil and professional challenges. The once familiar shores of safety and security were replaced by the treacherous waters of uncertainty. The workplace, a supposed sanctuary, became a battleground of its own, where I was met with indifference and a lack of support. But with my continuous championing with confidence, each challenge, once viewed as a mountain, transformed into a stepping stone in my journey. I picked up all incidents, which acted as a catalyst for personal growth. I demanded clarity from those around me, both personally and professionally. Problems remained, but my approach and attitude changed. With a newfound smile, I entered the office and returned home filled with gratitude. These wounds, once sources of pain, are now scars and symbols of my championing. They mark a path of growth that has tempered my spirit, testaments to a journey that has moulded me into a person I never thought possible.

So, how can we champion confidence in the corporate world?

- Mental Fortitude: A strong belief in one's abilities, resilience in the face of challenges, and a positive mindset are fundamental to building confidence.
- Physical Well-Being: A healthy lifestyle, proper exercise, and peaceful sleep are good combinations to improve our confidence in the corporate world. Through this, our brain can think in a better way and can become better at responding.
- Community Connection: Supportive relationships and a sense of belonging foster connection, not just with your own community but also with your workplace. I belong to different communities at work, like peer support and well-being communities.
- Talent Expansion: Mastery of new skills in the workplace and in life are equally important to boost confidence.
- Personal and Professional Goal Setting: Achieving milestones, no matter how small, reinforces self-belief.
- Positive Self-Talk: Replacing the self-doubt and negative self-talk with positive affirmations will elevate confidence.

Knowing the meaning of the acronym **'SILENT'** is a great practice I tried to add to my life in different ways: Serene, Intimate, Long-lasting, Empowering, and Nurturing tryst with my Creator.

- Serene: A sense of tranquillity and peace, allowing for inner reflection and introspection.
- Intimate: In the absence of noise and distractions, forge a deeper connection with yourself and your creator.
- Long-Lasting: Profound and long-lasting experience, leading to greater self-awareness, inner peace, and spiritual growth.
- Empowering: Allowing you to tap into your inner wisdom and strength.
- Nurturing: Self-care, nurturing your mind, body, and soul.

- Tryst: A transformative experience, revealing hidden truths about myself and my relationship with the divine.

I also started to love **KFC** – Kindness, Forgiveness, and Compassion.

The Power of Kindness, Forgiveness, and Compassion to Conquer Fear

- Kindness: By focusing on acts of kindness, we can shift our attention away from fear and towards positive emotions. Acts of kindness can create a ripple effect, inspiring others to do the same and fostering a sense of connection and belonging.
- Forgiveness: Holding onto grudges and resentment can fuel fear and anxiety. By practicing forgiveness, we can release negative emotions and create space for healing and growth. Forgiveness doesn't mean condoning harmful behaviour; it's about letting go of the past and moving forward.
- Compassion: Compassion involves understanding and sharing the suffering of others. By cultivating compassion, we can develop empathy, which can help us overcome our fears and anxieties. When we focus on the needs of others, we can gain perspective and realise that our fears are not as significant as we may think.

My daily tips to myself to be brave are:

Tip	Description
Start your day with mindfulness/ prayer	Practise meditation or prayer to calm your mind and focus on the present moment.
Find inspiration in true love	Let the power of love motivate you to be brave and overcome your fears.

Tip	Description
Trust your intuition/Spirit	Listen to your inner voice and trust you have the strength and wisdom to face challenges.
Be in the present	Focus on the here and now rather than dwelling on the past or worrying about the future.
Be mindful of others	Pay attention to the people around you and treat them with respect and kindness.
Honour everyone you meet	Recognise the inherent value and dignity of every person you encounter.
Trust in the divine	Believe that a higher power is guiding and supporting you in mysterious ways.

10 Affirmations to Conquer Your Fears

1. 'I'm brave and capable of facing my fears.'
2. 'Fear is just a feeling; it doesn't control me.'
3. 'I'm strong and resilient, and I can overcome any challenge.'
4. 'I choose courage over fear.'
5. 'I'm worthy of feeling safe and secure.'
6. 'I can trust myself to handle whatever comes my way.'
7. 'I'm releasing fear and embracing peace.'
8. 'My fears aren't real; they're just thoughts in my mind.'
9. 'I'm letting go of the past and focusing on the present moment.'
10. 'I'm surrounded by love and support, and I'm not alone.'

Remember, consistent practise is key to the effectiveness of affirmations. Repeat these statements daily, and believe in their power to transform your mindset and overcome your fears.

This is my best and **Inspiring** choice—**'I choose to believe that I'm the masterpiece of my Creator, and I'm the Princess of the King of Kings, my Father.'**

Chapter 6

Cooperative Synergy: Driving Shared Vision Through Collaboration

Cooperative synergy refers to the idea that when individuals or groups work together, they can achieve greater outcomes than they could individually. In the corporate world, fostering cooperative synergy among diverse teams, particularly those comprised of migrants, can lead to increased innovation, productivity, and overall success. **Collaboration** is a vital force that can empower migrant communities and help them overcome challenges. By working together, migrants can leverage their diverse skills, experiences, and perspectives to achieve shared goals and create a more supportive environment. While individual goals may diverge, a shared objective unites corporate teams. To achieve this shared goal, collaboration and a commitment to the collective effort are essential. But where should it start?

Collaboration is the cornerstone of strong family relationships. By working together, families can improve communication, share responsibilities, resolve conflicts more effectively, and create a supportive environment. When family members collaborate, they can achieve more than they could individually. They can build stronger bonds, foster resilience, and set a positive example for their children. Ultimately, collaboration is essential for creating a harmonious and fulfilling home life.

Three companies renowned for their success and innovation are Google, Microsoft, and PepsiCo. These organisations have demonstrated the power of collaboration to achieve extraordinary results. Larry Page and Sergey Brin, the co-founders of Google, built a company culture emphasising collaboration and innovation. Satya Nadella, the CEO of Microsoft, has transformed the company into a more collaborative and customer-focused organisation. As CEO of PepsiCo, Indra Nooyi fostered a culture of inclusion and collaboration, empowering employees and driving innovation within the consumer goods industry.

Martin Luther King Jr., Mahatma Gandhi, and Malala Yousafzai are also inspiring leaders who have demonstrated the power of collaboration and inspired me to do the same. King's leadership was rooted in nonviolent resistance, Gandhi emphasised cooperation and peaceful protest, and Yousafzai advocated for education and women's rights through collaboration. These leaders have shown us that great things can only be achieved through teamwork and cooperation. As Steve Jobs famously said, 'Great things in business are never done by one person. They're done by a team of people working together.'

The International Space Station (ISS), a joint project involving 15 countries, is a testament to the power of international collaboration. Similarly, the Global Fund to Fight AIDS, Tuberculosis, and Malaria demonstrates the effectiveness of global partnerships in addressing pressing health challenges. In the realm of healthcare, the World

Cooperative Synergy: Driving Shared Vision Through Collaboration

Health Organisation (WHO) plays a crucial role in coordinating international responses to health emergencies. These collaborations highlight the importance of working together to address complex global issues and achieve shared goals.

Speaking out about the current affairs of society in my hometown as a youngster, my dad used to think and wish that I would be a good speaker like him and confident enough to open up about the current issues in society. His dream was for me to become a great teacher who would inspire many and help others craft their lives and build their dreams. However, the experiences with cultural shifts after my marriage and moving out of the country with no family gave me a 360-degree change in my life where I became a naïve girl with no right to dream of her own life.

When I arrived in Australia with no dream of my own, I didn't feel connected to anything other than my own language and culture. My high need to have my mother tongue in my life, passion for my native language, love for speaking out, and desire to connect with the community fuelled my aspirations to start a radio show. One day, while attending a community event, I had an opportunity to start a community radio channel in our mother tongue and met three other Indian women who shared my passion for radio. We bonded over our love for music and culture and shared our experiences as migrants.

Inspired by a shared vision, we collaborated and created our own radio show, *MalayalaJalakam*. The program featured a mix of music, news, movie and book reviews, and talk segments discussing topics relevant to the Indian community in Australia. The show quickly gained popularity, attracting a loyal listener base. Over the years, we continued to collaborate, expanding our programming and reaching new audiences. We launched additional shows, covering topics such as Indian cuisine, cultural events, current affairs, parenting and tax tips for migrants, and children's programs to promote their tastes and cultural ideas. The platform became a hub for our community, providing a space for connection, celebration, and empowerment. Thirteen years later, the women's collaboration remains strong. Our radio show has become an integral part of the community in Australia, providing a platform for emerging artists, promoting cultural understanding, and fostering a sense of belonging. My dream of becoming a radio jockey has not only been realised but has also inspired countless others to pursue their passions, make a difference in their communities, and start similar shows.

Through collaboration within our migrant community, we established a group that provided a platform for cultural activities, personal growth, and social connection. As a member of this group, I had the opportunity to hone my public speaking and MC skills while participating in and organising various cultural events, such as cultural festivals and music performances. This experience was invaluable for my personal and professional development. Not only did I learn new skills and expand my network, but I also gained a deeper understanding of myself and my cultural identity. Collaborating with like-minded individuals from diverse backgrounds has been a truly rewarding experience. My passion for connecting with my spiritual traditions led me to seek out like-minded individuals and contribute to our community. Utilising my 11+ years of teaching experience, I was able to share my knowledge and wisdom with the younger generation. This journey of spiritual connection and mentorship has been incredibly rewarding.

The shifting tides of family dynamics forced me to temporarily distance myself from the community. This period of solitude, while initially painful, proved to be a catalyst for introspection. Removed from the distractions and noise of everyday life, I was able to engage in deep self-reflection. Many new migrants yearn for a connection to their cultural heritage. However, without a strong support network, it can be challenging to maintain these connections. Initial friendships may fade as people's priorities and aspirations evolve.

Cooperative Synergy: Driving Shared Vision Through Collaboration

I've witnessed this firsthand. Once seen as a source of inspiration, we can become marginalised as others climb the social ladder. It's a reminder that relationships, like life itself, are dynamic and subject to change. Migrants who arrived around the same time often share similar experiences and mindsets. Factors such as year of arrival, occupation, financial status, children, and community involvement can influence the dynamics of collaboration within migrant communities.

Understanding these shared experiences can foster stronger connections and facilitate effective collaboration among migrants. Through self-reflection, I realised that my initial focus on a single community was limiting my perspective. I had become too insular, believing that my chosen group was the only viable option. This narrow-mindedness hindered my ability to build broader connections and explore other opportunities within the migrant community. The lack of support and a growing desire for community led me to seek out new connections and explore other opportunities within the migrant community. It wasn't until the pandemic that I realised the importance of building a multicultural community, both personally and professionally. The isolation and challenges brought about by the pandemic forced me to re-evaluate my connections and seek out new opportunities for collaboration and support.

Transparency and open communication are fundamental to organisational success. While documentation is essential, fostering a culture of collaboration and knowledge sharing is equally vital. In the past, silos often hindered progress and innovation in the corporate world. However, recent trends like remote work and globalisation have encouraged a more collaborative environment. Collaboration isn't merely about sharing information; it's about harnessing the collective expertise of a team to achieve shared objectives. By working together, teams can enhance efficiency, elevate quality, and drive innovation.

To foster collaboration, organisations must create a supportive environment where employees feel safe to share their ideas and perspectives. This involves open communication channels, clear expectations, and a culture of trust and respect. By embracing collaboration, organisations can unlock new opportunities, drive innovation, and achieve greater success. In my experience, collaboration has been instrumental in driving innovation and improving patient outcomes within our healthcare team. By working together, we've been able to leverage diverse expertise and find creative solutions to complex challenges. While doing so, we need to make sure that we're following the five key principles of open communication, mutual goals, respect, flexibility, and shared responsibility, and we must avoid assumptions.

When Australian-born individuals use slang and informal language in professional settings, it can create a complex dynamic for migrants. This can be the core reason for the lack of collaboration in engaging in discussions or making decisions. My usual reliance on nonverbal cues, common in Indian culture, proved ineffective in Western professional settings. A particularly painful experience involved a failed presentation, where my inability to articulate ideas clearly led to public criticism. The pressure to conform, coupled with the weight of sole financial responsibility, eroded my confidence and forced me into a submissive role.

When my life experience impacted my passion, it changed my mindset, ignited my soul, and drove me to go forward in this life. My journey took a turn with a limitless yearning to lead and transform, igniting teams to connect the vast potential of self to catalyse positive change not just in the corporate world but in local communities. It started with the work within me to discover the real passion of my life. I slowly started to realise the 'Power of Communication, Collaboration, and Connection.'

My initial collaboration at work began with online conversations within our team. These virtual discussions provided a platform for us to connect, share ideas, and establish a common ground for managing our team's tasks and responsibilities during COVID time. Our virtual coffee catch-ups, online quizzes, and lunchtime data conversations provided opportunities for informal interaction and team building. These activities helped us establish a sense of camaraderie and foster a collaborative work environment. The increased demands of the healthcare sector during the pandemic highlighted the importance of collaborative teamwork. Our team established a more structured approach through virtual meetings and online platforms, leading us to adopt a matrix or functional team structure. This collaborative approach enabled us to navigate challenges and achieve significant project milestones and innovations successfully.

It's generally recommended to use standard English in professional settings to ensure inclusivity and effective communication. However, there may be situations where a limited use of culturally appropriate slang can be acceptable if it doesn't impede understanding or create a barrier for anyone. Ultimately, the key is to strike a balance between fostering a friendly atmosphere and maintaining professional standards. While the sense of exclusion and resentment experienced by migrants may not be immediately apparent, it can run deep. Beneath their outward appearance, they may be grappling with feelings of isolation and frustration. Even as we strive to promote multicultural diversity, it's essential to acknowledge the challenges faced by migrants. Despite their hard work and dedication, they may still experience discrimination, prejudice, and a sense of being marginalised. Addressing these underlying issues is crucial to create a truly inclusive and supportive environment for all.

Despite my desire to challenge authority and advocate for change, I often felt powerless and overwhelmed. The fear of repercussions and the unfamiliar corporate landscape made me hesitant to speak out. However, I eventually realised that remaining silent wasn't the solution. The weight of providing for my family forced me to suppress my voice and conform to the status quo. The fear of financial instability silenced my dissent, leaving me feeling trapped and powerless. This constant internal conflict eroded my self-esteem and confidence.

Inspired

After realising the rights and responsibilities of the employees in the organisation, I persisted in speaking up and advocating for change. While my initial efforts may not have yielded immediate results, I realised that collaboration with like-minded individuals could amplify our voices and create a more powerful impact. Collaboration is most effective when it's a two-way street involving mutual give-and-take. In the corporate world, transparency and trust are essential for building strong collaborative relationships.

These challenging experiences gave me the courage to rebuild, redefine myself, and embrace the unexpected. In the process, I unearthed a strength that far surpassed any adversity I've faced. I learned that Australian English is characterised by unique vowel pronunciations, a distinctive rhythm and intonation, and a rich vocabulary of slang and idioms. These linguistic variations can be challenging for those unfamiliar with the accent, especially given the regional differences that exist within Australia. To effectively communicate with Australians, it's essential to familiarise oneself with these linguistic nuances and adapt one's own speech accordingly. By doing so, you can enhance your understanding and appreciation of Australian culture and build stronger relationships with locals. Despite the challenges of transitioning from a language with 52 alphabets to English, I persevered. Building connections within different language communities, even if slow at first, proved to be invaluable in overcoming language barriers and adapting to my new environment.

While language barriers can present challenges, they shouldn't be seen as insurmountable obstacles to collaboration. Migrants often possess a unique ability to understand and adapt to different cultures. By recognising and appreciating this cultural fluency, we can foster stronger connections and build more inclusive communities. By engaging with different communities and colleagues at the workplace, I realised that acknowledging our cultural competence can boost our self-esteem and confidence, empowering us to

Cooperative Synergy: Driving Shared Vision Through Collaboration

overcome language barriers and contribute meaningfully to our communities. Collaboration is the key to breaking barriers in the corporate world. A mindset with openness and clarity is important to start this journey.

My collaboration with other corporate community members started through the area I love, yes, with the radio platforms. I started to connect with them, understand their life, and share with the community through the platform I love. I started to re-engage with the public speaking world through this collaboration.

Through years of navigating the complexities of the healthcare landscape, I witnessed firsthand the transformative power of evidence-based decision-making. I became a staunch advocate for the '3S' approach: Service, Science, and Sustainability. I firmly believe that these pillars hold the key to unlocking a healthier and more sustainable future. I recognised the transformative power of fostering a culture of camaraderie and support. Believing that by empowering teams, we could achieve extraordinary milestones, I joined a peer support group focused on well-being and diversity. I realised that organisations could create a positive and supportive work environment that fosters innovation, creativity, and high performance by empowering their teams.

Let us harness our collective passion to design a future brimming with innovation, sustainability, and compassion, guided by the power of Communication, Collaboration, and Connection.

My journey has led me to a profound realisation—true power lies not solely in data and innovation but in the transformative potential of the human spirit. I've discovered that true growth and fulfillment stem from personal development, self-discovery, and embracing our authentic selves. Through collaborative initiatives, I had the privilege of guiding my team and community members to discover their inner strengths and potential. Witnessing their growth and development was incredibly rewarding, fuelling my journey of self-discovery and fulfillment. This fresh understanding has inspired me to explore the interconnectedness of Soul, Self, and Status. I believe that by nurturing these three elements, we can unlock our full potential and create a more meaningful and fulfilling life. Collaboration starts in our soul first and then in our self. That's how I connected to different cultures, engaged with people with similar purpose and thoughts, and fought for a cause that my life **inspires** me to do. I collaborated with organisations, people, and initiatives that value respect, no violence, and the spreading of love, joy, and peace.

Key benefits of collaboration:

- Increased efficiency: By pooling resources and expertise, teams can accomplish tasks more quickly and effectively.
- Improved quality: Diverse perspectives and experiences can lead to better decision-making and problem-solving.
- Innovation: Collaboration fosters creativity and encourages the development of new ideas.
- Enhanced employee satisfaction: A collaborative culture can boost morale and job satisfaction.

In a world increasingly interconnected, collaboration isn't just a choice; it's a necessity. As migrants, we have a unique opportunity to bridge cultural differences and foster a more harmonious and inclusive society. By embracing cooperative synergy, we can create a brighter future for ourselves and generations to come. My journey as a migrant has taught me the invaluable power of collaboration. Through shared experiences, mutual support, and a holistic approach, we can overcome challenges, achieve our goals, and create a more fulfilling life. By embracing diversity, seeking opportunities, and connecting with our communities, we can make a positive impact on the world.

Cooperative Synergy: Driving Shared Vision Through Collaboration

Here are some practical steps you can take to foster collaboration and build strong relationships in your corporate environment:

1. Be Proactive: Seek out opportunities to collaborate with colleagues across different teams and departments. Volunteer for projects, participate in team-building activities and offer to assist with tasks outside your regular responsibilities.
2. Build Relationships: Take the initiative to get to know your colleagues on a personal level. Attend company events, join social clubs, or organise informal gatherings.
3. Communicate Effectively: Practise active listening, be clear and concise in your communication, and respect the perspectives of others.
4. Offer Your Expertise: Share your unique skills and knowledge with your team. This can help to build trust and respect among your colleagues.
5. Provide Constructive Feedback: Offer constructive feedback and suggestions to your team members. This can help to improve collaboration and problem-solving.
6. Be Supportive: Encourage and support your colleagues, even if they're facing challenges. A positive and supportive attitude can foster a strong sense of teamwork.
7. Embrace Diversity: Recognise and appreciate the value that diversity brings to the workplace. Be open-minded and respectful of different cultures and perspectives.
8. Foster a Culture of Collaboration: Encourage your team to work together towards shared goals and celebrate successes.
9. Seek Mentorship: Find a mentor who can provide guidance, support, and opportunities for growth.
10. Network Outside Your Team: Build relationships with colleagues in other departments and industries. This can help you expand your network and learn from others.

By taking these steps, you can become a valued member of your team and foster a more collaborative and inclusive work environment. I know that building strong relationships and collaborating effectively takes time and effort, but it's **inspiring** and the rewards can be significant.

Chapter 7

Commitment to Continuous Growth: *Future-Proofing Your Career*

When reflecting on the concept of commitment, I'm immediately drawn to a time when I poured my heart and soul into a particular endeavour at work in the world of data management. I became so engrossed in my work that I temporarily set aside other aspects of my life, focusing solely on achieving my immediate goal. I would often wake up early, prioritise work over all else, and dedicate countless hours to studying, researching, and exploring every facet of my chosen area of work. However, I eventually realised that this relentless focus on work wasn't conducive to a fulfilling life. The constant prioritisation of work over other aspects of my life created an unhealthy imbalance, leading me to question the sustainability of this approach. It was easy to commit time when I was alone with no kids.

Becoming a mother introduced significant challenges to my life, including the need to juggle numerous medical appointments and treatments. The emotional toll of motherhood was substantial, and I struggled to cope with the constant demands. I mistakenly believed I had to maintain a professional demeanour at work, even when emotionally overwhelmed. This led to a heavy burden as I carried the weight of my emotions into my professional life. However, I discovered that immersing myself in learning new technologies and exploring the world provided a refreshing mental break from the stresses of family and personal life. I was becoming more and more isolated at work while exploring more technologies. At the same time, the lack of transparency regarding workplace processes and procedures, coupled with insufficient guidance on how to perform tasks efficiently, often led to unnecessary workloads and inefficiency, which hindered my ability to contribute effectively and achieve optimal results.

My complete dedication to my family over 18 years ultimately led to the dissolution of my marriage. Faced with the challenges of single parenthood and financial instability, I realised that a significant change in approach was necessary to maintain my family's unity. As a single parent, I realised the importance of work-life balance. My children's well-being became my primary focus, and I understood that prioritising my own life was essential for their long-term benefit. I ultimately discovered a renewed sense of self and purpose.

Despite the challenges posed by the COVID-19 pandemic, including disruptions to daily life and the need for extended periods of isolation, I found a silver lining in the experience. The pandemic forced us to prioritise nature, personal health, and family connection. As we adapted to the new normal, we discovered innovative ways to work, interact, and celebrate together as a family. This newfound appreciation for quality time over quantity led me to commit myself more deeply to my family. By spending quality time together, we discovered the benefits of family collaboration and physical fitness. While the initial adjustment to a more active lifestyle was challenging, consistent

Commitment to Continuous Growth: Future-Proofing Your Career

effort and mutual support helped us establish a positive routine we all enjoyed.

I wanted to learn and connect with the right people to continue my personal and professional growth. My friend encouraged me to join the sessions run by Smart Inspiration UAE to identify the power of Thoughts, the power of Words, and the power of YOU. Connecting with these areas raised my awareness by identifying the connection between myself, my soul and my societal status. My mentor, Elizabeth Percy, who connects with me in different levels helped me to identify the needs of continuous growth and provided different tools for the the growth mindset. This journey had a great impact on my self-discovery. Her musical intelligence and decluttering of mindsets with music and intentional thought processes helped me commit to clear and continuous growth.

I started to listen to and engage with different podcasts, online sessions, and books. Embracing Mel Robbins' *Let It Go* philosophy catalysed my personal growth and positively impacted various aspects of my life. I incorporated these practises into my daily routine alongside my reading habit.

I let go of what I cannot control
I let go of the attachments that don't serve me well
I let go of worries that drain my energy
I let go of false expectations
I let go of resentment and anger
I let go of people who impact me negatively
I let go of negative feelings about myself

It was in the quiet moments, amidst the chaos, that I discovered a sense of peace. I learned to focus on what I could control rather than stressing over what I couldn't. By letting go of expectations and embracing uncertainty, I found a calm within the storm. To ignite my journey, I picked one of my friend's continuous motivations to join in the breathing exercise workshop and meditation. Her smiling face and active connections with people really attracted me to commit to the breathing workshops and spend time for myself on a regular basis. Along with that, I tried to get some inner healing studies and sessions through my Christian connections.

Gradually, I liberated myself from the chains of fear and anxiety, embracing freedom, peace, love, and joy. This marked the genesis of my newfound confidence. Recognising that confidence is a dynamic process, similar to the ebb and flow of an ECG, I embraced life's inherent dualities of joy and sorrow as indicators of continued growth.

I reignited a long-dormant passion for classical dance and music. Exploring various hobbies, including gardening, painting, and pottery, provided temporary solace during the pandemic. While many pursuits proved fleeting, my dedication to dance and music endured. These artistic outlets serve as a constant source of motivation and personal fulfillment. My classical dance (Mohiniyattaom) teacher's unwavering support and commitment have been instrumental in my ongoing dance journey. Her guidance has enabled me to master classical pieces and perform them on various stages, including at local community festivals. The profound sense of accomplishment and personal fulfillment I derive from these performances far outweighs any external recognition. The solid commitment demonstrated by my dance teacher serves as a powerful inspiration, motivating me to remain dedicated to my dance practice. Their dedication has instilled in me a strong sense of purpose and a determination to continue pursuing my goals.

My commitment to voluntary community radio shows was very close to my heart. I remember that when I was admitted to the hospital after an unexpected fall followed by a MET (Medical Emergency Team) call, I was organising the show over the phone. The bystander friend was following my instructions without any responses, showing their understanding of my attachment to the show. The radio is so

Commitment to Continuous Growth: Future-Proofing Your Career

connected to my life that the day I lost one of my triplets was the time I was running to my show on a Saturday morning, and my friend RJ had to cover for me. I was so committed to not missing the show as it was my connection to my culture and core. Starting my own radio show in an unfamiliar language was daunting, but my passion for connecting with others drove me forward. By sharing news with my network and gradually expanding my reach, I gained confidence, built valuable connections, and deepened my understanding of the diverse experiences of migrants in Australia. Now, radio is part of my identity and my place to share what I've learned and the best stories about my community. This is the time that helps me fill my own cup with positivity.

Inspired by these interactions, I became involved in various community initiatives, discovering a world of opportunities to contribute and grow alongside others. The confidence, connections, and content I'm sharing with other people have helped me learn more about different areas of migrants' life journeys in Australia. This led me to work with different initiatives that were available in the community. I was thrilled to find that lifelong learning was deeply ingrained in my own community, with exciting events like Wynnovation and Learning Festivals fostering a vibrant culture of knowledge sharing. Embracing this spirit of continuous learning, I began sharing my knowledge and skills by conducting masterclasses for young aspiring speakers. This rewarding experience not only enriched my own life but also empowered the next generation of communicators. It was a delightful experience.

While pursuing academic degrees to secure employment, I found myself lacking the motivation to apply the knowledge I had acquired. I felt a disconnect between the theoretical concepts I had learned and the practical application in the real world. This may be an issue with the Indian educational system, which prioritises academic achievement and theoretical knowledge over practical skills and real-world applications. I've discovered that a genuine love for learning is essential for effective education. Embracing a curious mindset and actively seeking knowledge allows us to truly internalise what we learn. Merely acquiring information without applying it in our daily lives renders the learning process futile. 'Love to learn and live' is my way of learning, and I helped people adopt this mindset, mainly the migrants who were struggling with a lack of freedom, self-esteem, and family violence.

To engage people in learning, I started to run online challenges in 2023. The first challenge I did was with 12 women, and we did 21 days of life transformation, learning to identify different areas of self discovery. Throughout these challenging days, we explored the seven wonderful powers of 'Self, Soul and Status.' We practised gratitude and shared our stories. We empowered each other and changed our focus to self-awareness, self-discipline, self-care, self-compassion, self-acceptance, self-improvement and self-efficacy in the first week. In the second week, we started to think about the ways to overpower guilt, shame, addiction, bondage, neglect, and anxiety and how we can cultivate purity and growth in our lives. In the third week, we connected to learn about commitment, compassion, community, communication, collaboration, and common sense. We concluded the session with three core points, 'Love, Joy, and Peace,' to create a heaven on Earth. We celebrated our lives with a mission to serve the people around us, come out of the four walls of uncertainty, build our dreams, and become the best version of ourselves. I'm so grateful to learn that these women are changing their lives for the better and making positive movements in their own areas. By modifying their own life through self-reflecting exercises, they make impacts not only in their personal life but also in the corporate world.

I went through a learning session during the Advent season in 2023 to cultivate my spirituality and faith with a community of around 60 people. We learned about diversity in faith and the core message of Advent and shared the learning over 30 days to celebrate Christmas. This welcomed different ideas to increase the continuous growth in my personal and professional life.

Commitment to Continuous Growth: Future-Proofing Your Career

The online challenge for men was another learning curve for me. 'March with Men' was a 21-day online challenge to educate our friends with guest speakers and learning sessions and learn about the need for awareness of sharing responsibilities and acknowledgment in the family relationship for continuous growth and advancement. The seven elements of well-being—self-acceptance, self-compassion, autonomy, environmental mastery, purpose in life, personal growth, and positive relationship—were the real learning I had to do by leading this session, and I realised that we always forget this in our busy lives. I'm so grateful for the respect and trust the participants and my male friends shared during this session.

Embarking on a sailing adventure in Melbourne with strangers, I discovered the transformative power of human connection. Engaging in meaningful conversations and sharing stories with my fellow sailors boosted my confidence and broadened my horizons. Intrigued by the diverse world of sailing, I delved into learning about different boat types, including yachts and catamarans, and even explored the fascinating lifestyle of those who live aboard vessels. This was my first micro-adventure as part of my continuous personal growth. It allowed me to take some of my program participants on a free sailing experience to improve their self-confidence. Their testimonials were really inspirational, like: 'It was such a wonderful and calming experience, it was really uplifting, it's lovely to know that someone cares about how we feel. Someone takes the trouble to do something to uplift our spirits. It's so humbling to realise that you take time out of your busy life to make us feel loved and cared for.' These words fill my life with love, joy, and peace and help me continue my commitment to continuous growth. And I learned the meaning of this quote, 'Let us not love with words or speech, but with action and in truth.'

I was touched by all the lives I was changing with simple but intentional involvement. I was embracing a lifestyle of lifelong learning. Exploring the thrilling journey of self-discovery through ongoing education and personal development, transforming challenges into opportunities for success. A valuable lesson I learned is the importance of prioritising consistency over quantity. It's not about the time spent but the continuous effort and dedication that leads to meaningful outcomes. So, I joined to learn about communities in Australia so that I could help my community better. I met beautiful people in this community from different cultural backgrounds, and it was the best place to learn about migrants and the problems they face. We encountered the fear, anxiety, and worries of being in a new world with no proper understanding of the diverse range of issues of the community. We were First Nations people, Australians, Maltese, Iraqis, Chinese, and Pacific Islanders, all from different age groups and gender norms. The generosity, openness, and authenticity of different people from this group touched me. The depth of hands-on experience in this safe environment where there's no competition was enormous. It was interesting to see that there weren't many Indian community members to learn from when I was studying. It was great to notice that the variety of teachers in the institute came from different backgrounds, and their passions and mindsets were varied even though they were making sure that there were no unconscious biases while teaching different topics like diversity, communication strategies, alcohol and other drugs, homelessness, etc.

We learned about intersectionality and implications in different areas, the stolen generation, the current impact of that generational trauma, and the areas in which the government is making changes. It's impactful to understand First Nations cultures and how the acknowledgment of the land helps us to love and respect the people around us. Family violence and how to respond to it was another eye-opener during this course. At the same time, even though I had experiences in alcohol-impacted communities, I didn't have much knowledge of the history of it. Alcohol was reportedly used 8000 years ago and opium 7000 years ago in ancient Mesopotamia, and the indigenous Australians chewed different types of plants to relieve hunger, tiredness, and pain. We found interesting ways of mining

Commitment to Continuous Growth: Future-Proofing Your Career

Bitcoins as well as how to be involved in community services and be an inspiration for many by helping in different ways.

The Motivational Interviewing Interventions—a counselling technique that helps people change by focusing on their own motivations—and their power in someone's life were in the learning areas and many different cultural norms, best remedies, and how to deal with community by respecting cultural diversity and inclusion. I regret that I didn't explore this area of study at the beginning of my life in this country. The answers to many of my questions were included in these studies, and this is the most valuable commitment I've made to improve my migrant life in Australia.

The mental health psychology first aid course I completed at my workplace was another great opportunity that helped me continue my commitment to that area. Continuous growth in your personal skillset is the way to future proof your career. As leaders in the corporate world, we should understand and learn how different cultural competencies work together to achieve organisational success. So with this investment in continuous growth, we're becoming the best leaders and understanding the company's strategy, the high growth areas in the organisation, and the influential people in the organisations. This will help you advance the corporate ladder by moving your goal according to changes in your personal interests. I'm keen to connect with diversity and inclusion in my workplace, and I'm actively seeking opportunities to learn more about this and explore the opportunities in those areas. I started to connect with well-being areas, initiated women's coffee time in our department, and started the Indian community in our organisation to help them be empowered with different involvements. Opportunities are always open if you're personally willing to work towards them. Your career will be safe if you're sharpening your life skills with continuous involvement in lifelong learning.

What are you doing to achieve continuous growth in your life? You may have a great, organised life, but being a busy migrant and full-time worker, you can easily assess your continuous growth. This can be your quarterly checklist.

5 Steps to Assess Your Continuous Growth:

1. Reflect on your personal and professional goals each quarter.
2. Track your learning—journaling is key.
3. Seek feedback—be open to constructive criticisms.
4. Measure your achievements—set new, challenging goals.
5. Stay curious and open-minded—foster a lifelong learning mindset.

Chapter 8

Competitive Growth Mindset: *Outsmart, Outplay, Outshine*

In the corporate world, the growth mindset is paramount. It's a crucial component that sets apart those who thrive from those who stagnate. We need to know how to ignite our ambition and learn how to harness competition as a catalyst for personal growth, pushing boundaries and striving for excellence while maintaining a healthy connection between the people around us with no rivalry. I experienced that for migrants, the growth mindset is particularly valuable. It allows them to navigate unfamiliar cultural landscapes, adapt to new challenges, and leverage their unique skills by accepting opportunities. By embracing a growth mindset, migrants can outsmart, outplay, and outshine their peers.

A growth mindset is essential for continuous learning and development. It's about recognising that skills and knowledge are not static but can be acquired and improved upon. In the rapidly evolving corporate world, staying stagnant is a recipe for obsolescence. I do remember that when I was in the same role with the same duties, it was so comfortable, but it was boring, and I didn't have any way to improve my skills and outcomes. The main lesson I learned is that a growth mindset isn't just about intellectual prowess but also emotional intelligence and interpersonal skills. It's about building strong relationships, fostering collaboration, and inspiring others. By embodying a growth mindset, you'll excel in your career and contribute positively to the organisations you work for.

Outsmarting involves demonstrating intellectual expertise, problem-solving skills, and a deep understanding of the industry. It's about showcasing your ability to think critically and creatively. Outplaying requires strategic thinking, effective communication, and a relentless drive for excellence. It's about consistently exceeding expectations and delivering results. Outshining means making a lasting impression, standing out from the crowd, and becoming a recognised leader in your field.

I never imagined that creating a personally fulfilling workspace was possible. The belief that technology would dictate my career path and limit my options seemed unshakeable. However, the post-pandemic corporate landscape has undergone a significant transformation, offering new possibilities for personal and professional growth. This helped me discover my personal passion in the workplace. I'm so grateful for the inevitable change that the pandemic enforced in many different lives around the globe.

Emotional intelligence, diversity, and inclusion have emerged as critical workplace topics after the COVID pandemic. My passion for these areas led me to explore ways to contribute meaningfully to my organisation. Through active participation in company initiatives and seeking out opportunities for personal development, I've been able to make a tangible impact. One such opportunity was a company-sponsored program that equipped me with the tools to identify and address the emotional needs of my team members. I started to learn human-centred design techniques, which weren't included in our curriculum when I did my master's studies. The area of focus was the connection between humans and making plans to connect with humans. In my case, that was patients. This experience deepened my understanding of leadership and ignited a passion for fostering a supportive and inclusive work environment. As a manager, I've been fortunate to align my values with the organisation's mission. By encouraging open dialogue, fostering collaboration, and empowering my team, I've witnessed firsthand the positive impact of a supportive workplace culture.

Creating a space where individuals feel valued, heard, and empowered isn't just a professional responsibility but a personal passion. It's a testament to the belief that work can be more than just a pay check; it can be a source of fulfillment and personal growth. The power of compassionate leadership cannot be overstated. When a team member is grieving the loss of a loved one, offering empathy and support can make a profound difference. By creating a safe space for open communication, I've been able to help my team members navigate difficult times and prioritise their well-being.

As a leader, it's essential to understand the personal challenges your team members may be facing. You can foster a supportive work environment that encourages open communication and collaboration by demonstrating empathy and compassion. This, in turn, can lead to increased productivity and job satisfaction. I've witnessed firsthand the positive impact of compassionate leadership. I've helped my team members balance their personal and professional lives by providing the necessary resources and flexibility. This has not only strengthened our team dynamics but has also fostered a culture of trust and respect.

While there may be criticisms and challenges along the way, the value of compassionate leadership is undeniable. By creating a supportive and inclusive work environment, we can empower our team members to thrive and achieve their full potential. The immense support I've received from my leadership team has been invaluable. Compared to the limited encouragement I encountered in earlier roles, the current level of support is truly exceptional. I've realised that it's essential to proactively seek guidance, explain my motivations, and demonstrate my passion and vision. By doing so, I've been able to effectively communicate how my efforts can benefit the entire team. I was so touched by my director's comments about my achievements in our teams, referring to the waves I'm making and encouraging others to witness my journey.

While challenges and differing perspectives may arise among team members, open and honest communication is key to fostering understanding and collaboration. I've learned the importance of empathy, compassion, and a willingness to see things from others' perspectives. By embodying these qualities, I've been able to create a more harmonious and productive work environment. I believe my peers would agree. There's always room for improvement, which is the slogan I'm working on.

I remember a time when I felt invisible, a mere cog in the corporate machine under the dungeon. My ideas were overlooked, and my efforts were undervalued. It was a crushing weight, a constant reminder of my perceived insignificance. Yet, amidst the despair, a flicker of hope ignited. I realised that my worth wasn't determined by others but by my actions. Embarking on a journey of self-reflection, I peeled back the layers of self-doubt and discovered a reservoir of untapped potential. I began to question my assumptions to challenge the narratives I had internalised. It was a painful process, but it was also liberating. I realised that my leaders' perceived neglect wasn't a personal attack but a reflection of my limitations. I needed to improve my communication skills, articulate my ideas more effectively, and make my value undeniable. I experienced that personal growth is the key to professional success.

Competitive Growth Mindset: Outsmart, Outplay, Outshine

With renewed determination, I immersed myself in learning, seeking out opportunities to develop new skills and expand my knowledge. I reached out to colleagues, building stronger relationships and seeking mentorship. As I grew, so did my confidence. I became more assertive and more proactive. I began to attract attention and be recognised for my contributions. I had gone from feeling invisible to being necessary to collaborate and contribute.

The lesson I learned is that our worth isn't defined by external validation. It lies within us, waiting to be discovered. By investing in ourselves, cultivating our skills, and nurturing our passions, we can overcome any obstacle, defy any expectation, and shine brightly in the world. I slowly learned that Mary Barra used to say, 'The most important thing is to be authentic to yourself. Don't try to be someone you're not.' My personal favourite Indra Nooyi's dialogue is, 'Don't be afraid to ask for what you want. You may not get it, but you'll never get it if you don't ask.' I'm telling myself each day that I won't allow others to tell me that I can't do things or don't belong, and I will work towards what I want with no fear.

While external factors can influence our careers, it's crucial to recognise the profound impact of our inner world. Often, when we feel undervalued or overlooked, we may attribute it to external circumstances. However, a deeper look reveals that personal growth and development are often the missing pieces. The real power and inspiration I'm getting in this journey is my great leader. I can connect with him in many ways while I'm in the corporate world. He was a great leader who preached and practised diversity and inclusion by choosing his twelve disciples from different backgrounds and building a great team.

Reflecting on my own career, I realised that my initial frustration with leadership were a reflection of my own internal struggles. By focusing on self-improvement, I was able to identify areas where I could grow and develop. This involved honing my communication skills, expanding my knowledge base, and cultivating a more positive mindset. This is what I learned through my 25 year corporate career—instead of dwelling on anger and frustration against the systems and people, focus on consistent self-improvement. Compete with yourself, striving to be better today than you were yesterday. Arrogance and self-centredness will hinder your progress. True success comes from personal growth and a genuine desire to make a positive impact. By focusing on your inner world and making meaningful changes, you'll attract opportunities and create a lasting legacy.

In many immigrant communities, there's a prevalent expectation that academic achievement and external validation are the keys to success. I was once caught in this trap, believing that the relentless pursuit of education and top grades would guarantee a fulfilling life. However, my migration journey shattered this illusion. The challenges I faced in my new country, from language barriers to cultural differences, forced me to re-evaluate my priorities. I realised that while education is valuable, it's not the sole determinant of success. Building meaningful connections, understanding my cultural identity, and fostering personal growth were equally important, if not more so.

I sought out support networks, joined cultural organisations, and engaged in self-reflection. These experiences helped me identify areas where I needed to grow and develop. By investing in myself, both personally and professionally, I overcame challenges and achieved my goals. I soon discovered that there was a vibrant community of migrants like me, facing similar struggles. We shared our stories, fears, and hopes. Together, we found strength and support. I learned about the numerous resources available to migrants, from government agencies to community organisations. There were people willing to listen, offer guidance, and help me navigate the complexities of my new life. Yet, I also realised that the journey of integration was largely a personal one. It required self-awareness, resilience, and a willingness to adapt. I had to identify my own strengths and weaknesses and find ways to leverage them in this new context. It wasn't always easy, but with perseverance and a positive mindset, I overcame the challenges and built a new life for myself. The key was to reach out, connect with others, and never give up on my dreams.

I learned that a competitive mindset isn't just about external achievements; it's also about internal strength and resilience. While education and qualifications are important, soft skills like leadership, communication, and emotional intelligence are equally valuable in the corporate world. By focusing on personal growth and developing these skills, we can position ourselves for success, regardless of our background or circumstances.

I yearned for a community where I could share my experiences and connect with others facing similar challenges. The corporate world often felt isolated, as many people couldn't relate to the unique experiences of migrants. I realised that creating opportunities was essential. Our organisation's commitment to diversity and inclusion provided a fertile ground for growth. I'm grateful that I could be part of the video series highlighting cultural differences, fostering a deeper understanding and connection among colleagues.

On Independence Day, I founded the Indian community within our organisation. The overwhelming response from fellow migrants was heart-warming. We shared our struggles, triumphs, and hopes. Together, we formed a support network that offered solace, encouragement, and practical advice. I discovered that personal growth and community building could go hand-in-hand. By creating a space for others, I was also empowering myself. The journey has been rewarding, a testament to the power of connection and the importance of giving back. If you're feeling isolated in the corporate world, remember that you're not alone. Communities are waiting to embrace you, and opportunities to make a difference right where you are.

The books that went through my reading lane gave me different insights. *The 7 Habits of Highly Effective People* by Stephen R. Covey provides a transformative guide for personal and professional success. It emphasises proactive thinking, prioritisation, effective communication, collaboration, and personal growth. Throughout *Outliers*, Gladwell illustrates the roles that a wealthy family, a strong community, and a dose of good luck play in an individual's achievement. On the other hand, he also highlights the idea that challenges can create opportunities that result in success. The most important lesson in the book is that it's important to follow your dreams and pursue your legend. Santiago's journey teaches us that we should never give up on our dreams, no matter how difficult the journey may seem.

In the context of migration, the ability to 'outsmart' the world often involves a combination of adaptability, resourcefulness, and cultural intelligence. We should overcome challenges and find opportunities to achieve economic success and social integration. This will help to outsmart the social barriers and help us make stronger connections to reduce isolation. The ability to outsmart is necessary to avoid exploitation in professional and personal situations and make sure that we're not losing our identity.

The key to successful integration lies in finding a balance between adaptability and cultural preservation. While 'outsmarting' the world can be a powerful tool, it's essential to maintain a sense of self and identity. Although many may not accept you or connect with you, don't worry about it because it's not their reality, it's yours. By combining cultural intelligence with a willingness to learn and adapt, migrants can navigate challenges and contribute positively to their new communities.

Outplaying is a catalyst for a growth mindset. It's more than just achieving success; it's a mindset that fosters personal and professional growth. Self-mastery is the hardest job you'll ever tackle, as we can be our best friend and worst enemy. All these readings tell one truth: whatever the mind can conceive and believe, it can achieve. It's essential to have faith that this desire will come true. Believing anything negative will cause the subconscious to translate the negativity into reality, sabotaging the final goal. So, a positive mindset is crucial for an outplaying personality.

In the corporate world, outplaying typically refers to surpassing one's peers or competitors in terms of performance, strategy, or execution. It involves a combination of skill, intelligence, and strategic thinking. For migrants, outplaying in the corporate world can present both opportunities and challenges. We can bring unique perspectives and experiences. The ability to navigate different cultural contexts and work environments can make migrants highly adaptable employees. Us migrants often have a strong desire to succeed and are willing to put in extra effort. The prejudice and discrimination in the workplace for migrants can be the problems we face while trying to outplay in the corporate world.

In order to be efficient in outplaying, migrants should make sure that they invest in developing technical skills and soft skills such as communication, problem-solving, and leadership. They also need good connections with colleagues, mentors, and industry professionals to expand their opportunities. They should be willing to embrace change and be ready to learn new things. They should always highlight their unique experiences and perspectives to differentiate themselves. By combining their skills, adaptability, and determination, migrants can outplay their peers and contribute significantly to their organisations' success. Why am I encouraging this? I wasn't aware of the ways we could improve ourselves, and I didn't do much in my own life. The lost opportunities never come back to us, so hold it and use it.

Migrants often bring unique perspectives, experiences, and cultural richness to the corporate world. Outshining isn't about being better than others; it's about reaching your full potential, making a positive impact, and leaving your mark on the world. You can truly outshine your peers by leveraging these strengths and adopting a strategic approach.

Why does outshining matter to me? It's helping me advance my career and increase my satisfaction level at my workplace. I feel like I'm helping people at work with my skill sets and passion. I'm inspired when other migrants make outstanding achievements, bring fresh ideas and approaches, and shape the culture in the corporate world. There are so few brown executives in my organisation, and I can see how efficient and competitive they are; they outshine to showcase their skills and expertise.

What am I doing to achieve this in my workplace? I'm not doing any magic; it's through simple strategies like understanding and appreciating diverse cultures, including my own and the corporate culture I'm in. I embrace change, always participate, and am willing to learn new things coming into the organisation. I invest in my professional development, stay up-to-date with industry trends, and foster a growth mindset by believing in my ability to learn and grow, even in the face of challenges.

It's highly important that we outshine at our workplace and work hard towards doing so because it's a sign of personal empowerment, and it boosts our self-confidence and personal satisfaction. We're representing our culture and providing a legacy for our families in this country. By excelling, migrants can inspire others and contribute positively to their organisations and communities. We're leading by example and taking our organisations to a higher end in diversity and inclusion. We're impacting our organisations for the better. Some people may think it's odd not having real need or authenticity in the initiatives you're doing, but you're rebuilding a nation.

What should we do as migrants to make this possible? That was my question during my emotional intelligence journey. So now, I'm sharing what I found and experienced during this journey with you.

1. Embrace Cultural Intelligence:

- Understand and appreciate both your own culture and the corporate culture you're entering.
- Be open-minded and willing to learn from others.

Competitive Growth Mindset: Outsmart, Outplay, Outshine

- Adapt your communication style and behaviour to fit different cultural contexts.

2. Build a Strong Network:

- Connect with colleagues, mentors, and industry professionals, both within and outside your organisation.
- Attend industry events and conferences to expand your network.
- Leverage your cultural connections to build relationships and gain insights.

3. Develop Your Unique Value Proposition:

- Identify your unique skills, experiences, and perspectives.
- Articulate how these can benefit your organisation.
- Find ways to differentiate yourself from your peers.

4. Continuously Learn and Develop:

- Stay up-to-date with industry trends and developments.
- Seek out opportunities for professional development, such as training programs and workshops.
- Be willing to step outside your comfort zone and try new things.

5. Foster a Growth Mindset:

- Believe in your ability to learn and grow, even in the face of challenges.
- Embrace setbacks as opportunities for learning and improvement.
- Set ambitious goals and strive for excellence.

By following these steps, you can develop the mindset and skills necessary to outsmart, outplay, and outshine in the corporate world as a migrant. Remember, success is a journey, not a destination. Stay focused, persistent, and believe in yourself.

10 Questions to Assess Your Growth Mindset in the Corporate World

1. Do you view challenges as opportunities for growth or as obstacles that hinder your progress?
2. When faced with setbacks, do you tend to give up, or do you persevere and find new ways to overcome them?
3. Are you open to feedback and willing to learn from your mistakes?
4. Do you set ambitious goals for yourself and strive to continuously improve?
5. Do you believe that your abilities can be developed through dedication and hard work?
6. Are you comfortable stepping outside of your comfort zone and trying new things?
7. Do you approach learning as a lifelong journey, or do you believe that your knowledge is fixed?
8. Do you focus on the process of learning and development rather than solely on the outcome?
9. Do you encourage and support the growth and development of others?
10. Do you believe that everyone has the potential to succeed, regardless of their background or circumstances?

If you answered 'yes' to most of these questions, it's a good indication that you have a strong growth mindset.

Chapter 9

Criteria for Promotion Clarified: *Your Career, Your Roadmap*

I had a winding career path in the corporate world, from education to healthcare to the private sector. My career journey began in the data world in an academic setting when I was trying to find a better job that had no direct communication with stakeholders. This led me to transition into the healthcare sector, where I found a better world focused on data. In my early days in healthcare, I delved into the world of data with the help of some fascinating peers. The new world of data and patient outcomes was both challenging and intellectually stimulating. I recognised that I needed to invest in my professional development to achieve my full potential. With renewed determination and a new dream, I immersed myself in the world of data technologies, eager to acquire new skills and knowledge. This experience sparked a curiosity about the broader business world, which was challenging and financially better, so I decided to explore opportunities in the private sector.

The transition to the private sector was a significant shift, with new challenges and expectations. The competitive landscape, the emphasis on results, and the fast-paced nature of the corporate world were a real contrast to the more patient-centred healthcare environment. Despite these differences, I found the private sector to be both exciting and rewarding. The interactions, opportunities, training, and implementation of new technology were really exciting. I learned how to progress in different roles and move around the organisation, doing technically challenging jobs that didn't involve severe direct stakeholder management. The cutthroat competition, unwavering focus on outcomes, and breakneck pace of the corporate world were inspiring; amidst these differences, I found the private sector invigorating and fulfilling.

My journey to career success wasn't paved with the support of influential mentors or powerful connections during these early days of my journey. I navigated the corporate world on my own terms, carving my path through sheer determination and hard work. While the absence of a 'godfather' presented unique challenges, it also forced me to develop a strong sense of self-reliance and resilience. Despite my outward success and my various roles, I was harbouring a deep-seated insecurity. Beneath the confident facade, I grappled with self-doubt and a lack of self-belief because of the lack of connections with the corporate world. While I thrived in different areas of my life, including family and community, my workplace performance was marred by internal personal struggles. The lack of connections to my own culture was the root cause.

The day of a great overnight migration of technology was a pivotal moment in my career. I was brimming with confidence, anticipating the accolades that would surely follow. Yes, all the technology migration was a great success. However, reality painted a harshly different picture. As I ascended to my 10th-floor office in the gleaming corporate tower, the once-vibrant atmosphere seemed muted. The cubicles, usually buzzing with activity, were eerily quiet. A sense of foreboding crept over me. A summons to a special meeting shattered my complacency. The HR department's faces etched with gravity delivered the devastating news: 'Bismi, I have to share the news that you're part of our second redundancy round.' The shock was palpable. I felt like a convicted criminal, stripped of my belongings and escorted out of the building with a cold, impersonal efficacy. I realised that, obsessed with the intricacies of my technical role, I had become blind to the broader organisational landscape. I was so engrossed in the day-to-day tasks that I lost sight of the company's overarching goals and mission. It was a profound rejection, a harsh awakening to the realities of the corporate world. The experience left me reeling, questioning my worth and place in the grand scheme of things. Overwhelmed by despair, I retreated into a shell of isolation. The thought of sharing the news with my family was unbearable. I contemplated drastic measures, driven by a sense of hopelessness and helplessness. It was my friend's unwavering support that pulled me back from the brink by reminding me that job loss, unfortunately, is a common occurrence in the private sector.

The global financial crisis of 2008 cast a long shadow over my career, job security became a paramount concern, and I found myself reassessing my priorities. As an IT professional, I should've been identifying the actions I could take during this time by seeking support, setting boundaries, utilising the flexible working arrangement, upskilling myself, and identifying my goals. But because of my lack of self-awareness and knowledge, or maybe a shameful mindset about job loss, I didn't seek any external help.

As a migrant mother with familial responsibilities, I realised the importance of finding a stable and supportive workplace. Unfortunately, my family's support during this difficult time was limited. The pressure to secure a new job and the potential consequences for my family forced me to make difficult choices, including missing my brother's wedding. After 25 years of migration, I realised that I had sacrificed precious moments with my family. The absence of shared experiences and the emotional toll of separation were far more painful than any other hardship I had faced. It was a wake-up call, a reminder that while career success is important, it cannot come at the expense of personal relationships.

The relentless cycle of interviews, resume modifications, and phone calls over those eight weeks was gruelling, yet transformative. It forced me to confront my fears, challenge my self-doubt, and emerge a stronger, more confident individual. I learned to be myself in interviews, articulate my value with conviction, and negotiate assertively. I applied for a variety of positions, regardless of whether I was a strong candidate. These experiences provided invaluable insights into the interview process and helped me develop my ability to articulate my qualifications effectively. That made a real difference inside me and reflected in the outcomes. By practising with real interviews, you can gain firsthand experience, build your confidence, and identify areas for improvement. You need to remember, every interview is an opportunity to learn and grow, regardless of the outcome.

Returning to the healthcare sector felt like a homecoming. My technical expertise and experience in data management proved invaluable in navigating the complexities of my area. While the pace was slower than the private sector, I found satisfaction in contributing to the well-being of others. While financial stability is important, I've come to realise that career satisfaction and stability are about more than just money. While my initial career aspirations were focused on personal growth and professional advancement, the realities of family life forced me to prioritise financial stability. The pace of innovation in healthcare was slower than in other sectors, hindering career advancement opportunities. Balancing family responsibilities with professional goals was challenging, limiting my ability to dedicate time to personal development, and years were gone with no real roadmap for me.

Criteria for Promotion Clarified: Your Career, Your Roadmap

I believed that pursuing a master's in business administration would provide a broader skillset and open doors to new career paths. However, while intellectually stimulating, the coursework felt disconnected from my immediate career needs. The time and energy invested in the degree didn't immediately translate into tangible career benefits. This experience taught me the importance of aligning education with specific career goals. While advanced degrees can be valuable, it's essential to consider the practical applications of the knowledge gained and how it can directly contribute to your career aspirations.

Despite my academic achievements, I lacked the confidence to advocate for myself and seek promotions or new opportunities. I waited passively for external circumstances to dictate my career path. It wasn't until the organisational restructuring that I realised the importance of taking initiative and advocating for myself. By embracing new roles and responsibilities, I gained valuable experience and started to develop my skills again. This experience taught me that career advancement often requires proactive steps and a willingness to seize opportunities. While certifications and degrees can be beneficial, they're not a substitute for effective communication, strong interpersonal skills, and a clear understanding of your career goals.

Proactively researching available roles within your organisation and identifying how your skills and experience align is a great way to start your internal movements. You need to tailor your communication to highlight your unique value and demonstrate how you can contribute to the organisation's goals. Supportive mentors can provide invaluable guidance and open doors to new opportunities. Building relationships with experienced professionals who can help you navigate your career path is critical to climb up according to your plans. Understanding and adapting to local cultural norms and communication styles can be crucial for success in the corporate world. Be mindful of cultural differences and strive to build strong relationships with your colleagues.

Navigating a corporate environment can be challenging, especially for migrants who may face biases and prejudices. It's important to be mindful of who genuinely supports you and who may be competing for similar opportunities. Sometimes, those you perceive as allies can turn out to be your biggest rivals. Building strong relationships and understanding people's motivations can help you navigate these complexities. It's easy to project our frustrations onto others, especially when facing challenges. We may perceive our managers as uncaring or unapproachable, but it's important to remember that they're also human beings with their own struggles. Behind the facade of authority, managers may be grappling with insecurity, stress, or a lack of understanding. By approaching them with empathy and understanding, we can build stronger relationships and foster a more productive work environment. Recognising our colleagues' diverse experiences and perspectives, including their cultural backgrounds and personal challenges, is essential for effective collaboration and communication. By approaching others with empathy and respect, we can create a more supportive and inclusive workplace.

When a manager is provided with inaccurate or misleading information about an individual, it can create significant obstacles. If they have favourites within their team, it can be difficult for those who are perceived as outsiders to gain recognition and opportunities. These factors can create a hostile work environment and hinder an individual's career progression. Your immediate manager plays a pivotal role in your career trajectory, so their support and guidance can propel your growth, while their lack of support can hinder your progress. Misunderstandings and assumptions can create significant barriers to career advancement and lead to ongoing frustration. Open communication with your immediate manager is essential for career growth and development. Sharing your thoughts, aspirations, and areas for improvement can foster a strong working relationship and provide valuable insights. You can overcome challenges and achieve your goals by demonstrating a commitment to continuous learning, patience, and perseverance. My personal experience has shown me the power of a positive mindset and the importance of building strong relationships with colleagues. **Remember, even in the corporate world, miracles can happen when we combine hard work, dedication, and a belief in ourselves with a positive mindset.**

As I walked my youngest twin to my office recently, I pointed out the imposing red brick building with its stone basement called stables. 'This is where the C-level executives work,' I explained. To my surprise, he replied, 'Why is it called 'stables'? Are all the bosses crazy animals?' His innocent question made me chuckle, but it also highlighted the truth that sometimes, they can be crazy and disconnected from the employee mindset.

As a middle manager, your relationships with peers, team members, and other teams can significantly impact your career growth. When you're the only migrant in a group, navigating these dynamics can present unique challenges. If your peers are unwelcoming or discriminatory, you may feel isolated and excluded from important discussions and opportunities. When your peers undermine your authority or challenge your decisions, it can erode your credibility and make it difficult to lead your team effectively. Again, when they're unwilling to collaborate or provide support, it can hinder your ability to achieve your goals. These are the most common experiences for a migrant in the corporate world.

You can only progress if you have good strategies, like seeking out opportunities to collaborate with your peers on shared projects or initiatives, demonstrating your competence, reliability, and integrity, communicating clearly and respectfully with your peers (even when you disagree), identifying the possible experts as mentors within the organisation who can provide guidance and support, and building good relationships with colleagues in other departments to expand your network and influence. While facing these challenges as a migrant, you need to work hard and smart to achieve your career goals.

As a migrant, I faced a multitude of challenges, including isolation from the community, family strain, and the emotional toll of navigating a new culture. These factors, combined with the demands of my management role, created a perfect storm of stress and uncertainty. While my organisation provided maternity support, I hesitated to share the full extent of my struggles. The fear of judgment and the potential consequences for my career kept me silent. Returning to work so soon after giving birth was a demanding task, but I felt a desperate need to regain my sense of purpose and financial stability by being a simple parent. I immersed myself in my work, hoping to find solace and distraction from my personal challenges. However, the physical and emotional turmoil of the loss of a child and the challenges of single parenthood had a significant impact on my well-being. This had a different impact on my professional advancement as well and I had to compromise on many levels.

Throughout my career, I've faced challenges and setbacks. There were times when my self-esteem and motivation waned. However, different personal incidents triggered me to sit back and work on my 'self'. I've learned the importance of perseverance, resilience, and a growth mindset. By focusing on my strengths, seeking growth opportunities, and maintaining a positive outlook, I've overcome obstacles and achieved my goals. No, I realised that my goals should align with my personal values. My career roadmap should reflect my authentic self. It's about finding meaningful, challenging work that aligns with your values. By prioritising personal growth, building strong relationships, and making a positive impact, I've found a fulfilling and rewarding career. I started to connect with other parts of the organisation, and connected more with cultural diversity and wellness. I learned more about community and mental health awareness. I started to connect with my own culture in the organisation and identified that people were having similar problems, such as bullying, discrimination, and lack of direction. I modified my expectations about my career goals and changed my roadmap to fulfill my life goals. I started to build my team with heart and helped them build their dream, becoming their support. I'm involved in the well-being of communities and spread the spirit of freedom and connection among overseas-born migrants.

While I may not be the most popular or well-liked among my peers, my primary focus is on my immediate team, my manager, and the organisation. My commitment lies in delivering a brilliant performance and contributing to the company's success. I may not have close relationships with all my colleagues, but I strive to maintain a positive and respectful mindset towards everyone and keep a good bunch of people along with a resilient spirit in me. Despite the challenges I've faced, I maintain a positive outlook and strive to do my best for my colleagues and the organisation. I believe in the power of kindness, empathy, and spirituality. I pray for the well-being of my colleagues, offering them my blessings and good wishes. I aim to create a positive and supportive work environment by focusing on my actions and intentions.

Climbing the Corporate Ladder: A Migrant's Guide to C-Level Success (Chief/Cultural Competency)

Achieving a C-level executive position, especially as a migrant navigating a new culture and professional landscape, is a significant accomplishment. Here are some key steps to help you on your journey:

- Be knowledgeable and skilled in your chosen field.
- Be a strong leader with excellent soft skills.
- Be intentional about building your personal brand.
- Be patient and persistent in your career journey.
- Be confident in your abilities and believe in your potential.
- Be respectful and professional in all your interactions.
- Be prepared to negotiate effectively and advocate for yourself.

By following these steps and staying focused on your goals, you can increase your chances of achieving C-level success as a migrant in the corporate world.

Revised Criteria for Promotions: A Migrant's Perspective

1. Cultivate Cross-Cultural Relationships: Build strong connections with established leaders who possess a cultural diversity mindset. Seek mentorship from individuals who can provide guidance and support, and open doors to new opportunities.

2. Prioritise Effective Communication: Consistently deliver clear, concise, and impactful communication. Adapt your communication style to different cultural contexts and ensure your messages are understood and valued.

3. Demonstrate Tangible Results: Align your work with the organisation's goals and deliver measurable outcomes. Quantify your achievements whenever possible to showcase your contributions and value to the company.

4. Foster Collaboration and Teamwork: Cultivate strong relationships with colleagues across different teams and departments. Demonstrate your ability to collaborate effectively and contribute to shared goals.

5. Align with Organisational Values: Demonstrate your commitment to the organisation's mission, vision, and values. Align your work with the company's strategic objectives and contribute to its overall success.

6. Leverage Your Unique Perspective: Highlight the unique skills, experiences, and perspectives you bring to the table as a migrant. Showcase how your cultural background can contribute to the organisation's diversity and innovation.

7. Develop Resilience and a Growth Mindset: Be prepared to face challenges and setbacks. Cultivate a positive mindset and a willingness to learn from your experiences.

By focusing on these criteria, you can increase your chances of career advancement and achieve your professional goals as a migrant in the corporate world. By combining exceptional performance with a commitment to cultural diversity and a passion for your work, you can significantly increase your chances of career advancement and make a lasting impact on the organisation.

Chapter 10

Constructing Clear Boundaries: *Setting Limits, Reaching Heights*

My world from 2000 to 2006 was a whirlwind of doctor's appointments, fertility treatments, and the crushing weight of my husband's disapproval. Each failed attempt at conception deepened the cracks in our marriage, his frustration manifesting in a relentless barrage of hurtful comments. 'Maybe if you were truer to yourself,' he'd sneer, his words laced with bitterness. 'This wouldn't be happening.' 'Maybe then we'd have a child,' he'd continue, his voice softening slightly. 'But we can't have a child or survive without money. I need stable finances and a baby, and for that, you need to do better.' The coldness in his voice and the bitterness in his words made me believe he was harbouring resentment towards me. I was walking on eggshells, anxiety and isolation a constant companion in the journey of becoming a mother.

Inspired

The financial abuse was insidious, a slow erosion of my independence. By controlling all finances, doling out an allowance that barely covered the necessities of my life, and even connecting with my own family. He questioned every purchase and scrutinised every receipt, his accusations of frivolous spending echoing in my ears. His resentment towards my infertility morphed into a suffocating grip on our lives. The worst impact was that he chipped away all my self-esteem. The weight of motherhood, coupled with the constant emotional abuse, felt insurmountable. I was suffocating inside our home's four walls. I wasn't ready to share the news with anyone, including my family, and I wanted to become a mother to disprove all judgments about me.

The behaviours like controlling your interactions with family, limiting your financial freedom, isolating you from others, and insisting on a 'we two, we one' mindset are all hallmarks of coercive control. This is a form of domestic abuse that often goes unrecognised, but it can be just as damaging as physical violence. Even though I was experiencing all these early in my marriage, I thought it was the model everyone followed and it was normal. I was told that the husband is the God, and we shouldn't be opposed to anything he says according to our culture. But later, I learned that it's part of coercive control and about power and domination. It's clearly stripping away your autonomy, making you feel dependent and isolated. This is a common practice in all Asian countries, especially in my home country.

My best friend pulled me aside the day I got married amidst the great cultural wedding celebrations and last-minute adjustments to my orchid flowers. Her eyes searched mine, a hint of concern clouding her usually cheerful face. 'Why have you changed 'your' style like this?' she asked, her voice soft but filled with an unspoken question. I stood there, encased in a wedding dress that felt like a costume. But it wasn't just the change in my clothes. It was the shift in how I engaged with others, a newfound hesitancy in my eyes that replaced my usual confidence, and the lack of genuine happiness that masked my true self. It was a silent conversation, held in the space between us, a testament to how well she knew the real me. I'm still wondering why I was moving out of my own life and changed to a different person. I needed to tell my dearest friend the truth. I *did* change, morphing into someone different to be the perfect wife, the ideal daughter-in-law, and the agreeable sister-in-law. All to ensure my husband's happiness...but at what cost to myself?

I recently learned a word that described something I'd been experiencing, and it was a revelation. Suddenly, I realised that what I thought was just me was a pattern, a shared experience. It wasn't just in my head. Even though I came out of the hardest relationships, I realised that for seven long years, I wasn't willing to dig deep to disengage from my old self and proclaim that I was over it. I was making myself busier with different responsibilities so I felt better and did things differently. But in the last three years, I've invested in myself to realise the truths I have to believe and practice.

Dr. Ramani often highlights that narcissism isn't just about vanity or self-love. It's a complex personality disorder characterised by:

- A grandiose sense of self-importance: Narcissists believe they're superior, unique, and deserving of special treatment.
- A lack of empathy: They struggle to understand or care about the feelings of others.
- A need for admiration: They crave constant praise and validation.
- Exploitative behaviour: They may use others to achieve their own ends without remorse.
- Entitlement: They feel they deserve special privileges and are above the rules.
- Jealousy and envy: They may resent the success or happiness of others.
- Arrogance and haughtiness: They often display a condescending attitude towards others.

- Sensitivity to criticism: They react poorly to any perceived slight or criticism.

All these may not be visible in one person, but some of them will be very prominent. This helped me find out the subtle ways narcissists can initially charm and captivate their partners, using love-bombing and idealised projections to create a false sense of intimacy. The narcissist's true colours emerge in later intimate relationships and in the corporate world as well by revealing their self-centredness, lack of empathy, and need for control. They may use gaslighting, blame-shifting, and emotional manipulation to maintain their power and keep their partners or team balanced. I learned that the long-term impact of narcissistic abuse can cause the erosion of self-esteem, feelings of isolation and confusion, and difficulty in trusting others in their life. This learning helped me identify the core issues I was experiencing in my life.

At work, I once received shocking feedback that my trust issues were affecting my decision-making. Though taken aback by such a personal comment, upon reflection and considering the impact of my past relationships, I realised that unconscious bias could indeed be influencing my choices. That feedback served as a wake-up call, prompting me to embark on the challenging journey of setting boundaries within my own thought processes. This marked the beginning of real change.

I established a fundamental rule: 'No means no,' and there was no room for interpretation. I had been overly accommodating, often assuming blame or fearing my actions' negative impact on others, believing it was my duty to feel or accept those burdens. But like a bitter fruit borne from my own experiences, I finally realised that I didn't need to carry the weight of other people's actions. Each adult must take responsibility for their choices, both good and bad. While triggers may exist, the actions that follow are one's own. This was a powerful lesson in establishing and maintaining healthy boundaries.

Constructing Clear Boundaries: Setting Limits, Reaching Heights

You shouldn't be overly concerned with how others feel; your priority should always be your own well-being and emotions. Practicing setting boundaries at home creates a solid foundation for extending those skills to the workplace. By establishing healthy boundaries within your personal life, you develop the confidence and communication tools necessary to navigate professional relationships with greater clarity and assertiveness.

I used to believe that true friendship meant sharing every aspect of our lives, being inseparable, and investing fully in a select few close friends. However, I've come to realise that this approach isn't always sustainable or healthy. Maintaining healthy boundaries is crucial for preserving the longevity and quality of friendships. While genuine connection and vulnerability are important, it's equally essential to recognise that we're all individuals with separate lives, needs, and experiences. Respecting those boundaries allows each person the space to grow, evolve, and maintain their own sense of self within the friendship. By establishing and communicating clear boundaries, we can ensure that our friendships are built on a foundation of mutual respect, trust, and understanding. This approach fosters a sense of balance and autonomy, allowing each person to feel valued and supported without feeling overwhelmed or suffocated. Ultimately, healthy boundaries can lead to deeper, more fulfilling, and longer-lasting friendships.

Establishing boundaries is undeniably challenging when you've never had them. The sudden shift can be jarring for both you and the people in your life. If you start asserting your needs and limits after years of being overly accommodating, it can lead to misunderstandings, conflicts, and even strained relationships. Some people might feel threatened or rejected by your newfound assertiveness, while others might struggle to adjust to the change in dynamics. It's essential to be patient and understanding during this process, recognising that it takes time for both you and those around you to adapt to the new boundaries you're setting. I truly believe that if our connection is genuine, even if misunderstandings or disagreements temporarily create distance, our true friendship will endure in their hearts and minds, acknowledged and cherished even in their silence.

Setting personal boundaries has a ripple effect extending far beyond your well-being. It positively impacts your family and your workplace as well. It will help you reduce the stress level at work. When you have clear boundaries, you're less likely to feel overwhelmed, resentful, or taken advantage of, leading to decreased stress and anxiety levels. Your expectations are related to these boundaries, and timelines can be managed through them. You'll also be able to focus more on your tasks and avoid burnout, leading to increased productivity. Setting boundaries at work encourages open and honest communication with colleagues and supervisors, fostering a more positive and collaborative work environment. I love to learn from our teams, and some of the simple acts they use to add boundaries in the hybrid working world include logging off after work, keeping their calendar busy during their lunch and break time, and adding clear out-of-office messages, and these are great examples that we can all practise.

Today, I vow to never again prioritise work over my well-being. In my early career, as a driven technical professional, I felt compelled to be constantly available, checking emails and reacting to every work-related notification, regardless of the hour or my personal circumstances. Even while on leave during my bout with COVID and amidst a work crisis, I couldn't resist the urge to jump in and fix things, believing it would be easier to handle myself. However, this relentless dedication ultimately backfired. My lack of boundaries led to harsh criticism about my communication and response times, significantly impacting my professional reputation. No one truly understood the extent of my sacrifices, working from my sickbed or neglecting my personal life. Today, I choose to prioritise my health and well-being, setting firm boundaries to ensure a healthier work-life balance. This is one of the key messages I pass to my team, and I always encourage them to delegate work.

Constructing Clear Boundaries: Setting Limits, Reaching Heights

Mastering the art of setting boundaries to achieve harmony between work and personal life is a crucial skill for anyone, but it's especially vital for single parents navigating the complexities of both worlds. The real actions to improve myself are the new goals and purpose, adding gratitude as an attitude in life, a sense of belonging, clearer priorities, and increased confidence. Moreover, the narrative of our life and purpose should be clearer and away from the pain we experienced before. It should be a healing journey, even if you need to be selfish for yourself while narrating your story a second time.

The core areas I'm concentrating on and choosing for me are:

- Self-care as a non-negotiable option by making time for activities that recharge me: This includes enjoying my radio show and having time with guests to recharge myself. Another method of self-care for me is attending church activities and being silent in front of my creator. I also concentrate on my dancing to get some healthy outcomes.
- Be with my family: Connect more with my boys and do the activities that they like. I was adding them to the activities that I liked before seeing the patterns in the community, but now choosing only ones they enjoy and respecting their identity.
- Be active at work and with the team: Creating opportunities to help the team excel in their tasks and goals.
- Build a support system: Connect with my core friends, walk and talk with them, and have connections with other community members who can offer emotional support and practical help.
- Utilise community resources: Explore options to share my ideas, skillsets, and motivation with others and community centres so they can provide support and enrichment for children.

How am I reaching heights along with my team? I need to invest in myself to be able to bring something to my team. Here are four key areas I regularly work on to set boundaries and invest in myself:

1. Self-Reflection & Prioritisation:

    - Identify Your Non-Negotiables: What are the absolute essentials in your personal life? Family time, self-care, hobbies? These are your sacred spaces, and protecting them is key.
    - Understand Your Work Commitments: Be clear on your job responsibilities and your company's expectations regarding work hours and availability.

2. Communication is Key:

    - At Work:
        o Be Clear and Assertive: Communicate your boundaries to your team and colleagues. Let them know your typical work hours and when you're unavailable.
        o Use Technology to Your Advantage: Set up out-of-office replies for emails and voicemails during non-work hours. Utilise 'Do Not Disturb/ busy' modes on your phone if needed.
        o Negotiate When Possible: If your job allows, explore flexible work arrangements like remote work or adjusted hours to better align with your personal needs.
    - At Home:
        o Set Expectations with Family and Friends: Let them know your work schedule and when you're available for social engagements.
        o Delegate and Outsource: Don't be afraid to ask for help from family and friends or

> > even hire help for tasks like cleaning or childcare if feasible.
> > o Quality Over Quantity: Be fully present when you're with your loved ones. Put away work distractions and focus on creating meaningful connections.

3. Enforce Your Boundaries Consistently:

- Say No When Necessary: It's okay to decline additional work tasks or social invitations if they encroach on your protected time.
- Stick to Your Schedule: Avoid checking work emails or taking work calls outside of work hours unless it's an absolute emergency.
- Don't Feel Guilty: Remember, setting boundaries isn't selfish; it's necessary for your well-being and overall productivity.

4. Adapt and Evolve:

- Regularly Re-evaluate: Your personal and professional life will evolve, so periodically reassess your boundaries and adjust them as needed.
- Be Flexible but Firm: There will be times when you need to be flexible, but don't let exceptions become the rule. Always come back to your core boundaries.

This is an ongoing process. It takes practice, self-awareness, and the courage to prioritise your well-being. By setting clear limits and communicating them effectively, you can create a harmonious balance between work and personal life, allowing you to thrive in both roles.

What I experienced as a migrant single mother wasn't known to me before, and I didn't have any place to connect to find out a better way. Single mothers are facing social isolation and discrimination from their own culture, and they're not willing or not aware of other areas of social gathering. Single mothers often face financial difficulties due to limited job flexibility and the high cost of childcare. Dealing with a toxic ex-partner, lack of supportive friends, and workplace challenges can take a significant emotional toll. Single mothers may experience stress, anxiety, depression, and loneliness even when they show strong faces outside. Despite facing numerous challenges, single mothers often demonstrate incredible resilience and strength. They develop coping mechanisms, build support networks, and prioritise their children's well-being. Over time, single mothers can find empowerment and growth through their experiences. They develop self-reliance, confidence, and a strong sense of purpose. How do I know all this? Because I've been a single mother for the last 12 years, raising my boys with no other financial support other than my corporate career.

Setting and maintaining boundaries is crucial for single mothers juggling multiple roles and responsibilities. It's about prioritising self-care, protecting your time and energy, and creating a healthy balance between work and personal life. At work, I learned to communicate clearly with colleagues and supervisors and started to advocate for flexible working arrangements as much as possible. I set clear expectations about availability and time commitments in family and community settings. My obligation mindset to attend social events changed and I learned how to be assertive. Another area is to have clear communication channels and boundaries around parenting responsibilities and interactions. The cultural clash of accepting a single mother is changing; maybe I should keep my viewpoints of getting embarrassed and accepting community involvement, especially those aligned with my core values.

I'm eager to share the importance of kindness, respect, and hard work, ensuring my kids grow up to be compassionate gentlemen. Yes,

Constructing Clear Boundaries: Setting Limits, Reaching Heights

I rebuilt my life, embracing my independence and creating a fulfilling career. I found love again in all I'm doing; I have goals to achieve and dreams to follow. I navigated the complexities of single parenthood in a foreign land, battling language barriers, cultural adjustments, and financial hardships. It was a journey fraught with challenges but also one of profound growth and self-discovery. Today, I stand as a testament to resilience, a beacon of hope for other women who dare to dream of a life beyond adversity. That is what helps me set effective boundaries.

Benefits of Setting Boundaries:

- **Reduced Stress and Anxiety:** Clear boundaries can help you feel more in control of your life and reduce feelings of overwhelm.
- **Improved Work-Life Balance:** By setting limits at work, you can protect your personal time and prioritise your well-being.
- **Healthier Relationships:** Boundaries foster mutual respect and understanding in your relationships with family, friends, and colleagues.
- **Increased Self-Esteem:** Setting and enforcing boundaries can boost your confidence and self-worth.

Chapter 11

Cultivating Career Aspirations: *Investing in Human Capital*

Career aspirations are your long-term vision for your professional life. They encompass the ambitions, goals, and dreams you hope to achieve throughout your career journey. Career aspirations are often rooted in your values, passions, and interests. They represent what truly matters to you in your professional life and contribute to a sense of purpose and fulfillment. They will change and evolve as you gain experience, discover new interests, or encounter different opportunities, but they should serve as a driving force, motivating you to strive for continuous growth and development. They provide a sense of direction and purpose, guiding your career choices and actions. They're unique to you as you're a unique masterpiece of your creator.

In the corporate world, human capital refers to the collective knowledge, skills, experience, and potential of an organisation's workforce. It's the intangible asset that drives innovation, productivity, and overall success. When employees are viewed as valuable assets rather than mere cogs in the machine, it fosters a culture of investment and growth. This shift in perspective can significantly impact career jumps, particularly for those who may face additional hurdles, such as migrants. Understanding the concept of human capital empowers you to recognise your own worth and advocate for your contributions, but it's often difficult to fully grasp your value from within the confines of your current role or perspective. An external, unbiased viewpoint, perhaps through mentorship or coaching, can be instrumental in identifying and highlighting your unique strengths and potential. This outside perspective can help you see beyond your current limitations, gain clarity on your career aspirations, and strategically position yourself for advancement. By collaborating with a mentor or coach, you can unlock the full power of your human capital and accelerate your journey towards career success.

For many migrants, the concept of mentorship can be a foreign and even intimidating prospect, often dismissed as an unnecessary expense or a luxury reserved for those with established careers. However, research has shown that mentorship can be particularly impactful for individuals navigating the complexities of a new culture and professional landscape. A mentor can offer practical career advice, emotional support, cultural understanding, and a sense of belonging in a potentially unfamiliar environment. Migrants often possess unique skills, experiences, and perspectives that can be immensely valuable to organisations.

Imagine having someone who understands your unique journey, who can guide you through the intricacies of the Australian workplace, decode unspoken rules, and help you bridge any cultural gaps. A mentor can serve as a sounding board, offering encouragement and reassurance during challenging times and celebrating your successes alongside you. This emotional connection can be crucial for migrants who may feel isolated or overwhelmed as they navigate a new culture and professional landscape.

While financial constraints are understandable, consider mentorship as an investment in your future, not just a monetary cost. The knowledge, connections, and confidence gained can open doors to opportunities you might not have otherwise discovered, ultimately leading to greater fulfillment and success. Embrace the possibility of mentorship, not as a burden but as a powerful tool to help you realise your full potential and thrive in your new home.

I was fortunate enough to be surrounded by experienced and expert individuals within my industry, yet I failed to actively seek their insights or advice on career growth and progression. My conversations with them remained confined to general community matters, completely separate from my professional aspirations. I mistakenly assumed that since our specific areas of expertise didn't perfectly align, they couldn't offer valuable guidance. However, I've realised the immense value of connecting with those within your community, even if their career paths differ slightly from yours. They possess a wealth of knowledge and experience that can be invaluable in navigating the corporate landscape. Identifying and engaging with the right individuals within your community can provide you with mentorship, support, and access to hidden opportunities. Their insights can illuminate potential career paths, offer strategies for advancement, and provide valuable feedback on your professional development.

Identifying and connecting with communities that prioritise career growth is crucial for anyone seeking guidance and support in their professional journey. These communities can serve as invaluable resources, offering insights, mentorship, and opportunities for advancement. I realise my error in confining my network to familiar cultural and social circles, thereby missing out on opportunities for broader connections and diverse perspectives that could have significantly enriched my professional journey.

Mentorship is a powerful tool for personal and professional growth. By connecting with experienced individuals who can provide guidance, support, and advice, you can accelerate your career and achieve your goals. A mentor can help you with the following areas:

- Career advancement: Mentors can provide guidance, support, and opportunities for career growth.
- Skill development: Mentors can help you develop new skills and knowledge.
- Increased confidence: A mentor can boost your confidence and belief in your abilities.
- Networking opportunities: Mentors can introduce you to valuable contacts in your industry.
- Personal growth: Mentors can help you develop as a person and achieve your goals.

By building strong relationships with a mentor, you can unlock your full potential and achieve your career aspirations. Remember, the key to a successful mentorship is open communication, mutual respect, and a shared commitment to growth and development.

Mentors can come in various forms, each offering unique benefits and perspectives. Here are some common types of mentors:

1. Formal Mentorship:
    - Company-Sponsored Mentorship Programs: Companies often organise these programs to match employees with mentors based on their career goals and interests.
    - Industry Mentorship Programs: These programs connect individuals with experienced professionals in a specific industry or field.

2. Informal Mentorship:
    - Peer Mentorship: Mentorship relationships between peers who are at similar stages in their careers.

- Reverse Mentorship: Mentorship relationships where a less experienced person mentors a more experienced individual.
- Community Mentorship: Mentorship relationships within a community or volunteer organisation.

3. Executive Mentorship:
    - Mentorship relationships between senior executives and junior employees.

4. Virtual Mentorship:
    - Mentorship relationships that are conducted primarily through online communication tools.

5. Self-Directed Mentorship:
    - Mentorships where individuals seek out mentors independently, often through networking or research.

The type of mentorship most suitable for you depends on your needs and goals. When choosing one, it's often helpful to consider the mentor's experience, expertise, and personality.

Initially, I was hesitant to dive into the world of mentoring, but I took a leap of faith and started with the Victorian ICT for Women network, an industry-driven initiative aimed at supporting women entering the IT field. They run a program called Go Girl, Go for IT, and I had the opportunity to volunteer my time to help out. The network also offered coaching programs to support us on our journeys. The various guest speakers and activities were instrumental in fostering my growth mindset and inspiring me to embrace mentorship. My first mentor was an inspiring figure, the founder of a thriving IT organisation. I was captivated by her drive and vision, but in retrospect, I realise I missed a crucial opportunity to fully benefit from her guidance. At that time, I lacked a clear goal or direction for my own career. This lack of focus prevented me from fully absorbing her wisdom and applying it to my own professional journey.

The conferences I attended broadened my horizons and provided valuable insights into potential areas where seeking a mentorship could significantly accelerate my growth and development. However, a turning point came when I enrolled in a comprehensive seven-month program for women leaders offered by Women and Leadership Australia. This program equipped me with the skills, behaviours, and mindset necessary to step into senior roles and opened my eyes to the diverse possibilities of coaching and mentoring. In those pre-COVID days, face-to-face interactions allowed me to connect with potential mentors and coaches on a deeper level, where I truly grasped the distinction between their roles and how they could support my journey.

Mentoring and coaching, while often used interchangeably, offer distinct approaches to professional development. Mentoring typically involves a long-term relationship where a more experienced individual (mentor) shares their knowledge, insights, and experiences with a less experienced individual (mentee) to guide their overall career growth. On the other hand, coaching is a more structured and goal-oriented process, where a coach helps individuals develop specific skills or overcome specific challenges to achieve defined outcomes.

In the fast-paced and competitive corporate world, a blend of both mentoring and coaching is often the most effective approach. Early in your career, mentorship can provide invaluable guidance and support as you navigate the organisational culture and establish your professional identity. As you progress, coaching can help you refine your skills, address specific performance gaps, and achieve ambitious career goals. By leveraging the strengths of both mentoring and coaching, you can maximise your potential and accelerate your journey towards success.

Cultivating Career Aspirations: Investing in Human Capital

During the challenging period of COVID, my focus shifted towards family well-being and navigating organisational complexities. This period of introspection led to a profound personal evolution, where my interests expanded into mental health, multicultural awareness, inclusion, and diversity. My goals transformed as I felt a calling to become a speaker, sharing my experiences and insights with both the corporate and community worlds. I began actively networking, attending free conferences, and seeking out opportunities to connect with like-minded individuals. This proactive approach fuelled my personal growth and opened doors to potential speaking engagements and collaborations, bringing me closer to my newfound purpose.

Unaware of the financial commitment involved in the new mentoring or coaching world, I attended a major conference hosted by JT Foxx and Ethan Donati. Their enthusiasm for creating change in the world was palpable, and I was struck by the sheer number of people who seemed to have access to instant financial success and the opportunity to become renowned speakers. Witnessing this firsthand triggered a shift in my thinking. As a single mother, my income felt stagnant, leaving little room for personal investment in my human capital. Yet, I knew deep down that it was time to prioritise myself for personal growth and to improve my family's financial stability. I dreamt of speaking up and sharing my story, but I was held back by the limiting belief that I lacked the necessary resources.

Standing at that conference, surrounded by seemingly endless possibilities, I felt a pang of frustration. How could I pursue my dreams without the financial means to invest in myself? But just as doubt crept in, a fellow attendee approached me, curious about my story. As I shared my struggles as a single mother and my burning passion for speaking, a flicker of hope ignited within her eyes. She then extended a life-changing invitation: a free five-day challenge designed to help aspiring speakers find their voice. At that moment, something shifted within me. I realised that despite financial constraints, growth and transformation opportunities still existed.

With newfound determination, I embraced the challenge, embarking on the next chapter of my speaking journey. From that moment on, I dedicated myself to honing my speaking skills and opening up a world of networking and connection. I took a leap of faith and made financial investments, hoping to make remarkable life changes.

I can attest to the profound benefits of embracing spirituality, both personally and professionally. From my perspective, mentorship has been a guiding force throughout history, evident in the lives of countless successful leaders who sought wisdom and support from trusted advisors. The concept of mentorship is not new; it's been woven into the fabric of human experience since time immemorial, transcending cultural and religious boundaries. The Holy Bible is filled with examples of powerful mentorship relationships that highlight the profound impact of guidance and support on personal and spiritual growth. These stories served as a source of inspiration for seeking to develop meaningful mentor-mentee connections.

- Moses and Joshua: Moses, a seasoned leader, invested significant time and energy in mentoring Joshua, preparing him to take on the mantle of leadership. This mentorship ensured a smooth transition of power and the continued success of the Israelites.
- Elijah and Elisha: Elijah, a powerful prophet, took Elisha under his wing, imparting his wisdom and spiritual gifts. This mentorship empowered Elisha to continue Elijah's legacy and the prophetic ministry.
- Paul and Timothy: Paul, a seasoned apostle, mentored Timothy, a young and eager disciple. Their close relationship fostered Timothy's growth as a leader and evangelist, enabling him to establish churches and spread the Gospel.
- Jesus and the Disciples: Jesus, the ultimate mentor, invested deeply in his 12 disciples, teaching them, guiding them, and empowering them to carry on his ministry after his ascension.

Cultivating Career Aspirations: Investing in Human Capital

These biblical examples demonstrate the transformative power of mentorship. They showcase the importance of investing in others, sharing knowledge and experience, and fostering a supportive environment for growth and development. These principles remain relevant today, reminding us of the profound impact we can have on others by offering guidance, encouragement, and belief in their potential.

Mentoring and coaching are undeniably powerful tools for personal and professional growth, but their effectiveness hinges on a few crucial factors. First and foremost, you need to have a clear goal, a well-defined system, and unwavering commitment. Without these, mentorship or coaching can become a fruitless endeavour. Furthermore, your goals and values must align with those of your mentor or coach. If there's a disconnect, speaking up and seeking alternative guidance is crucial. Forcing a mismatched relationship can be detrimental to your self-worth, confidence, and even your finances.

In today's world, the notion that 'good mentors always come with a hefty price tag' is simply untrue. There are numerous free yet valuable mentoring and coaching opportunities available, as well as paid options with varying degrees of success guarantees. Regardless of the path you choose, the key is to actively work towards your core goals, recognise your own value, and be prepared to adapt and adjust your commitments along the way. Remember, the journey of self-discovery and growth requires dedication, resilience, and a willingness to invest in yourself, both personally and professionally.

Building strong professional relationships is undoubtedly crucial for career advancement, but networking with intention is where the true magic happens. It's not just about attending industry events or connecting on LinkedIn; it's about fostering genuine, one-on-one connections with people who share your passion and ambition. These personalised interactions offer a deeper level of engagement and understanding, allowing you to exchange valuable insights, uncover hidden opportunities, and cultivate mutually beneficial relationships. Remember, the seeds of future collaboration and success are often sown in the quieter moments of authentic conversation. So, make time for those meaningful one-on-one conversations, whether it's a coffee catch-up, a virtual chat, or a simple phone call. By investing in these personal connections, you'll be well on your way to achieving your career goals and creating a network of support that will last a lifetime.

Building strong professional relationships through intentional one-on-one conversations is crucial for career growth. However, these connections need to translate into tangible actions and impact within your workplace to truly make a difference. If you're not actively applying the insights gained and opportunities discovered through networking or not sharing your newfound knowledge or advocating for yourself and others, then those connections remain untapped potential, a waste of valuable time and energy.

> To ensure that your networking efforts yield meaningful results, consider these ways to showcase your commitment and drive at work:
>
> - **Share insights and knowledge**: Offer to present key learnings from conferences or networking events to your team, demonstrating your initiative and willingness to contribute to the collective growth.
> - **Advocate for yourself and others**: Use your expanded network to champion your own ideas and projects and support and elevate the voices of colleagues who may be facing barriers or challenges.
> - **Initiate collaborative projects**: Leverage your connections to explore opportunities for cross-functional collaboration or innovative initiatives that benefit the organisation.

- **Seek mentorship or sponsorship opportunities**: If you've connected with inspiring leaders, express your interest in learning from them and seek their guidance as mentors or sponsors.
- **Demonstrate continuous learning and growth**: Apply the knowledge and skills acquired through networking to your work, showcasing your dedication to professional development and your willingness to adapt and evolve.

By actively integrating your networking efforts into your professional life, you'll demonstrate your commitment to growth, create tangible value for your organisation, and build a reputation as a proactive and impactful contributor.

Discover the power of mentorship by uncovering the secrets to building meaningful relationships with mentors and coaches who champion your career and elevate your professional journey. As a middle-level manager, I possess a unique opportunity to benefit from my mentorship and foster a culture of growth and development within my team by instilling a similar mindset about human capital. By recognising the value of each team member's skills, experience, and potential, I'm creating an environment where individuals feel empowered to invest in their own growth and pursue their career aspirations. I encourage the team to seek out mentors or coaches who can provide guidance, support, and advocacy, helping them navigate challenges and unlock their full potential.

You can lead by example, sharing your own mentorship experiences and highlighting the positive impact it has had on your career. Offer opportunities for your team members to connect with experienced professionals within the organisation or industry, facilitating meaningful mentorship relationships. Furthermore, consider incorporating coaching elements into your own management style. Provide regular feedback, set clear expectations, and offer support and guidance to help your team members achieve their goals. By fostering a culture of continuous learning and development, you'll cultivate a motivated and engaged team that's committed to its own growth and the success of the organisation. You need to realise that as a middle-level manager, you have the power to inspire and empower those around you. By embracing mentorship and coaching, both for yourself and your team, you can create a ripple effect of positive change, unlocking the full potential of your human capital and propelling your team and organisation towards greater success.

When organisations invest in their teams through mentorship, coaching, and professional development initiatives, they reap numerous benefits that extend beyond individual growth. High employee retention rates, increased productivity, and a positive work environment are just a few of the outcomes. By fostering a culture of continuous learning and support, organisations can experience a significant boost in revenue, cultivate happier and more engaged employees, and foster a strong sense of teamwork and collaboration. This holistic approach to employee development benefits individuals and strengthens the organisation as a whole, creating a win-win scenario for everyone involved.

We've witnessed how embracing a growth mindset, seeking guidance from experienced individuals, and aligning our actions with our core values can propel us towards fulfilling our career aspirations. From recognising the transformative power of mentorship to acknowledging the unique challenges faced by migrants in navigating the corporate world, we've unearthed a wealth of insights into unlocking our full potential. We should learn that career success isn't solely about climbing the ladder but also about finding meaning, purpose, and alignment with our deepest aspirations.

By continually investing in our human capital, fostering meaningful connections, and remaining true to our core values, we can navigate the complexities of the corporate world with resilience, purpose, and unwavering commitment. Let us remember that our journey of growth and development is a lifelong endeavour, fuelled not only by our own determination but also by the **inspiration** we draw from others.

Chapter 12

Commemorating Achievement: *More Than Milestones, a Celebration of You!*

'If you start life as an immigrant, you first want to find out the community of your origin that will help you to learn the ropes of this new world.' These insightful words came from my 11-year-old twin boy, advice I sorely missed when I arrived here in 2000. His ability to offer such wisdom speaks volumes about his understanding and compassion, and it was a proud moment for me as a mother. Raising sensible, thoughtful boys is an achievement I cherish deeply. It's a testament to the values I've instilled in them and the example I've set. For me, true success lies in living a life guided by strong values and taking action towards the causes I care about. These principles form the bedrock of my decision-making, guiding me towards a life of purpose and fulfillment.

Inspired

I've come to realise, perhaps later than I should have, that celebrating every precious moment in our lives, whether big or small, is essential for fostering joy and gratitude. This includes savouring accomplishments in our personal lives, cherishing quality time with family, appreciating the connections we forge within our communities, acknowledging milestones in our careers, and recognising the fruits of our labour in business ventures.

Every achievement, no matter how seemingly insignificant, serves as a stepping stone for growth and a testament to our capabilities. Let us celebrate these moments not just as fleeting triumphs but as opportunities to reflect on our progress, acknowledge our strengths, and fuel our motivation to strive for even greater heights. Remember, the knowledge and skills gained from each accomplishment can be transferred and applied to new challenges, empowering us to continuously evolve and make a lasting impact in various spheres of our lives.

Over the years, my technical expertise and unwavering dedication to my work have been met with recognition and opportunities for growth. I'm particularly proud of my gradual evolution from an individual contributor to a team leader, where I now have the privilege of mentoring and guiding a talented group of IT professionals. As a leader, I'm deeply passionate about empowering my team members to achieve their career aspirations. My collaborative approach and supportive leadership style create a positive and productive environment where everyone feels valued and encouraged to thrive.

When I embarked on my career in database management, working in a literal basement—our IT department was relegated to the hospital's depths for seven long years—I had no grand dreams or aspirations. Little did I know that success would manifest as a vibrant department of over 50 multicultural and brilliant IT professionals, housed on the fourth floor of a modern building adjacent to a state-of-the-art facility. This transformation represents a remarkable achievement not just for

Commemorating Achievements: More Than Milestones

our team but for me personally. As a leader, I've been both motivated and humbled, learning invaluable lessons about leadership while guiding three diverse teams. I've also had the privilege of contributing to areas beyond my technical expertise, offering peer support, promoting well-being, raising awareness about family violence, and fostering a sense of belonging within our multicultural community.

As someone who initially sought data-driven community connections through meetups and conferences, evolving into a role where I actively share ideas as a speaker and engage with the media represents a significant career success. My journey has been one of transformation: from a technically focused individual concerned with backups and troubleshooting to embracing a management mindset where leadership is seen not as a single leap but an ongoing evolution. I'm constantly seeking the sweet spot where data-driven insights intertwine with cultural diversity and inclusion, leading to extraordinary outcomes. Shifting from casual conversations about family violence to sharing my personal story on online platforms and in-person stages, both within the community and corporate world has required immense courage developed over a lifetime. Engaging in organisational activities to promote employee well-being and awareness has been a fulfilling quest to uncover meaningful results. Seeing my message and courageous photos displayed on the walls of my workplace after three years serves as a powerful validation. It's a reminder that my journey wasn't just recently ignited; it's been a long, often silent, but determined path.

Becoming a middle-level manager is undeniably challenging, yet it also presents a golden opportunity for learning and growth. I'm proud to share that I've actively sought out training sessions that have significantly shaped my career trajectory, contributing to my overall success.

One particularly impactful experience was the 360 Leadership Assessment, a comprehensive evaluation that illuminated my strengths and areas for improvement. The feedback I received from various stakeholders provided invaluable insights into their perspectives, prompting me to adapt and refine my leadership style. I vividly recall the debriefing session with the external consultants, where their comments about my leadership deeply resonated with me. Their observation that I 'identify options for my team leads strategically and efficiently, showcasing great leadership skill sets' profoundly affirmed my efforts. It remains a milestone that I continue to celebrate, a reminder of my growth and potential.

In the corporate world, fostering collaboration and celebrating collective achievements are paramount. I firmly believe in acknowledging and celebrating each milestone in our journey as a team. Our nominations for the Excellence Award for Emerging Leaders and Collaborative Team within our organisation are a testament to this shared success. Being recognised in a healthcare-clinician-specific industry, where visibility can be challenging, makes this achievement even more meaningful. I'm truly proud of my progress and the positive impact I've had on my team and organisation. It's a testament to the power of continuous learning, self-reflection, and a genuine commitment to fostering a supportive and collaborative work environment.

My own experiences as a migrant have given me a deep understanding of the unique challenges faced by those navigating the corporate world in a new country. As a result, I actively use my position to champion diversity and inclusion, fostering a welcoming and supportive environment for all team members. I'm incredibly proud to be part of the Indian community within our organisation, a space that facilitates cultural exchange, mutual support, and valuable networking opportunities. By connecting with employees from diverse backgrounds, I'm actively contributing to a more inclusive and collaborative workplace, one small step at a time.

My passion for public speaking has opened doors to numerous opportunities to share my experiences and perspectives on various

Commemorating Achievements: More Than Milestones

national and international platforms. I've delivered impactful talks on topics close to my heart, such as migration, culture, personal growth, motherhood, disability, inclusion and diversity, family violence, work-life balance, and environmental well-being. Sharing these stories on both national and international stages has been a fulfilling journey, marking a significant success in my pursuit of a meaningful speaking career.

While my journey in emceeing began in 2008, confined to my cultural community and mother tongue, today I proudly grace a variety of stages, captivating audiences from diverse faiths, cultures, and corporate backgrounds. It's a testament to my growth and versatility as a communicator.

I'm truly grateful for the opportunity to leverage my skills as a session leader and event organiser, serving both community and corporate clients. Facilitating workshops, conducting training sessions, and moderating engaging discussions on diverse topics bring me immense joy. I relish in utilising my natural charisma and talent for emceeing and hosting radio shows, creating memorable experiences for attendees and listeners alike.

My most cherished success, one I hold close to my heart, was emceeing an event for Tiffany Hunter, my dear First Nations friend and first mentor who ignited my passion for public speaking. It was her end-of-year function, celebrating the vibrant tapestry of multicultural communities. We revelled in the diverse flavours of food and the warmth of genuine love from a community that wholeheartedly encourages us to pursue our dreams.

I also treasure the deep connections I've fostered in both the corporate and community worlds. Over the past three years, I've had the privilege of connecting with over 300 individuals from various walks of life. My current focus is on identifying these relationships' core essence and underlying purpose. I firmly believe that cultivating meaningful connections can profoundly impact our lives, opening doors to new opportunities, fostering personal growth, and creating a sense of belonging and support.

A major triumph in my community service endeavours has been the wealth of knowledge I've gained over the past two years. I was previously unaware of the many beneficial programs and initiatives the council and community offer residents. Being part of the largest council in my city, one with a rich tapestry of multicultural residents is a source of great pride and accomplishment.

Sharing my personal story for the first time within my council was a significant milestone, another victory to cherish. My 13-year involvement with community radio has been incredibly fulfilling, allowing me to host two distinct shows that showcase my cultural heritage, faith, and connections. Last Mother's Day season, I had the privilege of featuring daily stories throughout the month of May, highlighting 32 remarkable mothers who are also award-winning entrepreneurs. My radio platform has become a space to amplify global narratives and local heroes' inspiring stories. It's particularly gratifying to know that some of my guests experienced their very first live radio interviews with me, empowering them to continue sharing their voices and stories. These experiences reinforce the profound impact of community engagement and storytelling, and I'm deeply grateful for the opportunity to contribute to my community in this meaningful way.

Volunteering for a worthy cause is always a fulfilling endeavour, and I'm deeply grateful for the opportunity to contribute my skills to exceptional podcast platforms dedicated to spreading love, joy, and peace. Nurturing my spiritual well-being and connecting with my core values remains a cornerstone of my personal success. The radiant love and unwavering devotion demonstrated by those serving the Lord is truly contagious, its power resonating throughout the world. Even the simple smiles shared by the wise souls in aged care homes as I spend precious time with them become treasured moments of success and connection.

Simultaneously, the empowering moments spent with the Young Emerging Speakers, sharing laughter and growth during our training sessions, mark another cherished milestone in my journey. Witnessing the transformation of different people as they embrace their unique voices and develop their public speaking skills fills me with immense pride. And shouldn't I celebrate the mere opportunity to conduct my masterclasses in person, a platform that has attracted diverse groups of adults and children eager to learn and grow?

Overcoming my deep-seated fear of water has been a significant personal triumph worth celebrating. Though the root cause of this fear remains elusive, I'm immensely grateful to this beautiful country for providing me with the opportunity to learn to swim and conquer this lifelong obstacle. The confidence of knowing I can stay afloat has opened up a world of possibilities. It's empowered me to step outside my comfort zone, even sailing with strangers, a feat I once considered unimaginable. This journey of overcoming fear has been incredibly empowering, reminding me that with determination and support, we can conquer any challenge that stands in our way.

Finally driving to our capital city was a dream realised, a milestone I joyously celebrated with my family. Embarking on long drives alone with my three boys also marked a significant personal victory over years of accumulated fears and anxieties. These seemingly ordinary adventures symbolised a newfound freedom, a testament to my courage and determination to craft a life where I could embrace both independence and cherished moments with my loved ones. Celebrating these small milestones along the way served as a powerful reminder of my resilience and the boundless possibilities that lie ahead.

My love for dance and music remains a constant source of joy and self-expression. I actively participate in dance classes and cherish the opportunity to perform in various cultural events. I'm immensely grateful to my guru for recognising and nurturing my passion for classical art forms, which has led to the incredible achievement of performing on different stages. Similarly, my passion for music has propelled me to delve into the world of classical music. While still learning, I consider it a significant success that my teacher believes in my potential and encourages me to continue singing. These artistic pursuits enrich my life and provide a fulfilling outlet for creativity and self-discovery in my special way.

My thriving garden is a success story I proudly celebrate and share. Connecting with friends over my garden has been a wonderful experience, fostering a sense of shared passion and community. Sharing the experience of attending flower shows with friends and discovering new and exciting plant varieties has been a truly enriching and delightful journey. The abundance of pumpkins, plums, apples, tomatoes, and lemons brings immense joy and satisfaction, not only to me but also to the community members with whom I generously share the harvest. The delicate white jasmine flowers, blooming in profusion, symbolise the beauty and celebration that fill my life. Their fragrance and presence uplift my spirits and create a serene ambiance in my backyard. And then there's my beloved pet, a seven-year-old chicken who brightens my mornings with her cheerful greetings. Her unwavering loyalty and companionship are a constant source of encouragement and solace, reminding me of the simple pleasures and great connections that enhance my backyard haven.

My greatest source of love, joy, and peace is my family. Witnessing my sons flourish and achieve their dreams fills me with immeasurable pride and contentment. My eldest, the heart of our family, possesses a remarkable maturity that I cherish as a precious gift. My twins, blossoming into confident teenagers, bring me unique joy and purpose. We celebrate every milestone, big or small, recognising the significance of their efforts and achievements. Whether it's their dedication to reading, acts of kindness at school, diligently completing chores, offering tech support to their IT professional mother, or even creating entertaining YouTube videos, each accomplishment is acknowledged and appreciated.

Having true friends who are willing to initiate open conversations about my actions and point out any perceived lack of authenticity is a blessing worth celebrating. It signifies genuine care and a desire for personal growth. Their constructive feedback serves as a valuable mirror, reflecting aspects of myself that I may not fully recognise. This willingness to engage in honest dialogue fosters a deeper level of trust and intimacy within our friendships, and I'm grateful for their presence in my life.

Yes, saying NO to people, situations, actions, and thoughts are big successes if you're living with no boundaries. I'm learning this slowly, but I celebrate my small successes in this area with high importance. The decision to stay away from loved ones is hard, but if it's a good cause with great value, I consider it a success. Living alone with no support is hard, but seeing your family thrive is a cause of celebration and gratitude.

This doesn't mean that I did it all by myself. I had massive help from a very special handful of people in my life. Some of them have gone away from life for valuable reasons, and some are within my reach if I need them. But I'm learning to be closer to my core than others, which is the success I love to celebrate. Amazing blessings from people who care about me, and my cause is helping me. My mother is a powerhouse of prayers for our family. My loving brothers and their family helps me grow. To me, it's a great success to celebrate.

My celebrations are a vibrant tapestry woven with moments of joy, connection, and appreciation:

- Family: Surrounded by the laughter and love of my boys, we indulge in a feast of flavours, sharing stories and engaging in

> meaningful conversations. Movie nights stretch into the wee hours, and we find solace and wonder in nature's embrace.
> - Friends: Adventures and experiences create lasting memories as we explore new places and savour the warmth of good company over steaming cups of coffee or food.
> - Corporate: The rich aroma of Melbourne coffee fills the air as we celebrate achievements and toast to future successes.
> - Personal: Tranquillity washes over me during quiet moments of reflection, phone calls filled with laughter, and heartfelt emojis. Gratitude fills my heart as I embrace the blessings of each day, finding peace in silent nights. Walks in nature rejuvenate my spirit, and I celebrate the successes of others with genuine enthusiasm.

At the core of every celebration is a deep sense of worth and contentment. I feel blessed to have a life filled with love, laughter, and meaningful connections. Each celebration is a reminder of the beauty that surrounds me and the joy that resides within.

I find deep resonance in the words of St. Francis of Assisi, who wisely said that building a dream requires patience and persistence, laying each stone, day by day. Small beginnings, nurtured with heartfelt effort, can blossom into remarkable achievements. My story may not seem as grand as others, but it's a testament to the transformative power of acknowledging one's truth, even in the face of adversity. My life, marked by abandonment, has taught me to find beauty and strength in the smallest of things, recognising that they can become the foundation for extraordinary accomplishments. It's slowly growing into an inspired life.

I believe my life's purpose lies in sharing my story with you, a testament to the indomitable power of resilience, determination, and the unwavering human spirit. I've overcome countless challenges, embraced unexpected opportunities, and positively impacted my community through unwavering faith in my own spirit. My true success, however, is the conviction that any migrant, anywhere in the world, can achieve anything they set their mind to if they connect with their inner strength and purpose, combining hard work, dedication, and a positive, grateful attitude.

If you're reading these words, it's a victory worth celebrating. Your interest in my story fills me with hope, and I'm confident you'll share its message with others.

Is success in the corporate world simply about climbing the ladder? Is it solely defined by promotions, securing the highest bonus, or reaching the coveted C-level executive positions? Or could it be something more profound, encompassing personal fulfillment, work-life balance, meaningful contributions, and continuous growth? How do you define success in your own professional journey, and how does it align with your core values and aspirations?

You can decide and define your success, but it shouldn't be just on the corporate side of your life. It should be the celebration of YOU. Success isn't a one-size-fits-all concept. It's not just about climbing the corporate ladder or accumulating wealth. True success is about living a life that's meaningful to you, one that aligns with your values and brings you joy. It's about overcoming challenges, growing as a person, and positively impacting the world around you.

My journey has been far from easy. I've faced numerous mental and emotional challenges and health challenges from anaphylaxis and asthma attacks to cerebral palsy and cerebral aneurysm surgeries. I've spent countless hours in hospitals and therapy sessions, and I've had to adapt to a life of single parenting with no financial support. But these challenges haven't defined me. Instead, they've made me stronger, more resilient, and more appreciative of the good things in life. They've taught me the importance of perseverance, gratitude, and compassion. I've learned that success isn't about what you achieve but who you become along the way. It's about the lessons you learn, the relationships you build, and the impact you have on others.

Learn how acknowledging and sharing your achievements, both big and small, can create a ripple effect that inspires others. By recognising your progress and celebrating your successes, you fuel your motivation and ignite the spark within those around you, encouraging them to pursue their dreams with renewed passion. In turn, as you witness others celebrating their victories, their enthusiasm and drive can become a source of inspiration for you, creating a cycle of mutual encouragement and support that propels everyone towards greater heights.

As I close this chapter of my life, I'm filled with gratitude for my experiences, the people I've met, and the lessons I've learned. I'm proud of the person I've become and excited about the future. I hope my story **inspires** you to define your own success, celebrate your unique journeys, and never give up on your dreams. Remember, you're the author of your own story. You have the power to create a meaningful, fulfilling, and joyful life. If you need a helping hand to succeed, let's partner to create a personalised roadmap to success. Reach out to me today and let's get started!

So, start celebrating YOU! Youthful Optimistic Unleasher!

My greatest success lies in the **inspiration** of the simple act of breathing, a testament to the Creator's purpose within me. Each breath is a celebration of life, an opportunity to fulfill that divine purpose, echoing the words of Genesis 2:7, 'Then the Lord God formed a man from the dust of the ground and breathed into his nostrils the breath of life, and the man became a living being.'

About the Author

Bismi Palatty is a first-generation migrant who has called Australia home since 2000. She is a Speaker, Facilitator, Radio Producer, Host, MC, and founder of DomminnusNissi Social Impact Platform and YES (Young Emerging Speakers) Academy to help first time speakers. She is an advocate for disability, Inclusion and human empowerment. She heads the Data Platforms and Integrations team for one of Melbourne's major state-wide healthcare providers. Her passion for multicultural diversity and inclusion is spreading to the corporate world, allowing her to identify the gaps in the migrant mindset. She is on a mission to champion diversity and inclusion, igniting a powerful movement in the community and the corporate sphere.

She gives priority to helping her three boys to be resilient and speak up for them. To continue a similar goal in her community, she shares her time through YES Academy which aims to help people become better speakers and advocates for themselves. Her radio platform showcases people who spread love, joy, and peace. She spread these core values through her speaking engagements, facilitations and other community participation. Her true belief is, that 'connecting to the core is the beginning of change' and helps others to connect to their core purpose.

Bismi Palatty
Speaker, Author, MC, Coach & Radio Host

Bismi is a passionate Power-Speaking Coach who empowers individuals in the corporate world to find their voice and speak with confidence. She fosters a supportive and encouraging atmosphere, drawing on her personal experience to help professionals connect with their core values and confidently share their perspectives, leading to a greater impact and contribution within their organisations. Bismi provides practical tools to help professionals articulate their ideas, advocate for themselves, and contribute meaningfully to their teams.

TOPICS

- **Mastering the Corporate Pitch of Persuasion for Professional Success:** Crafting and delivering compelling presentations and proposals that achieve your objectives
- **Connecting with Your Communicative Core:** Clarity, Confidence, and Connection for Authentic Leadership Presence
- **Building Communication Resilience Through Crucial Conversations:** Practical strategies for navigating high-stakes, emotionally charged conversations and setbacks with confidence
- **Strategic Communication:** Asserting Your Perspective Respectfully for Optimal Outcomes with clear, direct, and diplomatic communication in professional settings

 bispalatty@domminnusnissi.org   facebook.com/bispalatty
 0401360144   bispalatty
 bismipalatty   domminnunissi.org

Notes

Inspired

Notes

www.ingramcontent.com/pod-product-compliance
Lightning Source LLC
Chambersburg PA
CBHW020417080526
44584CB00014B/1378